McGraw-Hill
Mathematics

English Language Learner Handbook

2

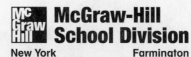

McGraw-Hill School Division

New York   Farmington

McGraw-Hill School Division

*A Division of The **McGraw-Hill** Companies*

McGraw-Hill School Division
Two Penn Plaza
New York, New York 10121-2298

Printed in the United States of America

ISBN 0-02-100292-4

1 2 3 4 5 6 7 8 9 047 05 04 03 02 01 00

GRADE 2 Contents

ENGLISH LANGUAGE LEARNERS HANDBOOK

The purpose of the *English Language Learners Handbook* is to provide support to teachers with students for whom English is a second language. The Handbook includes assessment tools with follow-up activities as well as language and concept-development activities correlated to each chapter in *McGraw-Hill Mathematics 2001*. The *English Language Learners Handbook* consists of the following sections:

- Language-Free Math Inventory (pages 2–4)
- Essential Math Vocabulary Inventory (pages 8–11)
- Teaching Essential Math Vocabulary Pages (pages 12–20)
- Cluster Activities (pages 21–95)

The two inventories assess the mathematical and language abilities of students acquiring English. The **Language-Free Math Inventory** assesses the mathematics ability of students based on standards for children at the previous grade level. The **Language-Free Math Inventory** measures students' familiarity with key mathematics vocabulary. Key vocabulary includes words that students are typically expected to comprehend at the beginning of a given grade level. In addition, the inventory assesses directive language such as write, cut, circle, cross out, and underline. The **Teaching Essential Math Vocabulary Pages** offer suggestions to meet students' needs based on their responses on the Essential Math Vocabulary Inventory. Each item on the Inventory has specific instructional strategies on the Teaching Pages.

The majority of the pages in the Handbook comprise **Cluster Activities** language- and concept-development activities that are correlated to the chapters in McGraw-Hill Mathematics 2001. These activities incorporate all concepts introduced in the student textbook with strategies and techniques to help students move through the various stages of language acquisition toward fluency in English.

Strategies That Support English Language Learners

When planning activities for students, be alert to students' varied levels of language. While the stages of language acquisition are predictable, individual progress through the stages varies. A brief discussion of the five stages of language acquisition follows.

Stage 1/Pre-Production: Students have very few oral skills; however, they may be able to respond by pointing, gesturing, nodding, or drawing.

Stage 2/Early Production: Students listen with greater understanding and can say some English words, phrases, and simple sentences. The types of questions that students respond to best are yes/no, either/or, and listing-type questions.

Stage 3/Speech Emergence: Students can understand written English that includes pictures, objects, actions, and sounds.

Stages 4 and 5/Intermediate and Advanced Fluency: At stage 4, students are able to use more extensive vocabulary, demonstrate increased levels of accuracy and correctness, and express thoughts and feelings. At stage 5, students are able to produce language comparable to native English speakers.

The strategies listed below offer general suggestions for teaching all ages of students acquiring English.

- Create a print-rich environment to model English.
- Create a math word wall by organizing a bulletin board for flash cards that can be displayed alphabetically. Each flash card would contain a key mathematics term students are learning.
- Label classroom materials and objects; for example, pencil, scissors, table, chair, desk, chalkboard, sink, light switch, and so on.
- Encourage students to use manipulatives as often as possible.

- Use real-life objects or models whenever possible; for example, when discussing word problems involving people, show small plastic figures.
- Provide students with prompts. Using prompts gives students a model for correct syntax and focuses their attention on the content of what they are trying to say. Prompts differ according to the question being asked; for example, if you give students this problem, "3 frogs are by the pond. 2 more frogs hop up. How many frogs are there in all?" a possible prompt would be "There are ____ in all." Students fill in the blank with their own ideas, such as, "There are 5 frogs in all. (The use of realia, or real objects, would increase student understanding of the problem. The use of a prompt increases the likelihood of students responding aloud.)
- Encourage students to use masks and puppets to speak for them to help alleviate some of the stress as they begin to speak out in class.
- Beginning in second grade, have students create their own Math Words Dictionaries. Each student makes or receives a booklet made by stapling together 14 sheets of paper. The top sheet becomes the front cover. The remaining sheets are lettered with the alphabet, one letter per side of paper. Then, as the student learns a new mathematics word, he or she writes it on the page that matches its initial letter. The student then uses pictures and his or her own words to define the word. As more words are learned, the student adds them to the booklet.
- Tape record story problems for students to listen to and solve. Make copies of the problems so students can follow along or read aloud as they listen.
- After completing an activity, challenge students to come up with a rule or concept they have learned. Write it on the board or on a sentence strip for students to read aloud.
- Incorporate all learning modalities, including visual, aural, and tactile.

How to Use the Cluster Activities

The **Cluster Activities** in the *English Language Learners Handbook* incorporate each concept introduced in the student textbook of *McGraw-Hill Mathematics 2001* with strategies and techniques to help students move through the various stages of language acquisition toward fluency in English. It is important to keep in mind that language acquisition is an individual process and that not all students will progress through the same stages at the same rate.

Each chapter in the Handbook is organized into two clusters that mirror the chapters in the student textbook. Each cluster begins with a list of clearly stated objectives, the materials you and students will need, and a chart of essential math words with examples or suggestions for presenting them. As you work through the activities with students, encourage them to use the math words in context. Questions and prompts often appear within an activity to facilitate vocabulary usage. For additional ideas, see Strategies that Support English Language Learners above.

Meaningful and engaging hands-on activities and manipulative materials promote involvement, interaction, and communication with peers while helping students to move from mathematical concepts that are simple and concrete to those that are more complex and abstract. You can easily modify the activities to meet the individual needs of your students. After completing each activity, encourage students to summarize and share what they have learned with you, a partner, or a group of peers.

HOW TO USE THE LANGUAGE-FREE MATH INVENTORY

The **Language-Free Math Inventory** assesses the mathematical ability of incoming students at the previous grade level and is taken independently by each student. The purpose of this tool is to focus on mathematics knowledge without involving language. The Inventory assists the teacher in identifying English language learners who are behind cognitively either because they have not had the opportunity to attend school or have not received specially designed academic instruction while learning English.

The items included in the **Language-Free Math Inventory** are based on mathematics standards for students at the previous grade level. The results will reveal who may need remediation. For example, if a student inaccurately responds to or skips two or three sections, you will know where he or she needs help. If a student is unable to complete accurately more than half of the items, you might want to engage him or her in remediation, according to your school's or district's philosophy.

The **Language-Free Math Inventory** is taken independently by each student. All English language learners could complete the inventory at the same time as you monitor them without giving assistance. So that students do not feel overwhelmed, it is suggested that you have them complete one page at a time with breaks in between or over a period of days. As students begin the Inventory, explain that you do not expect them to know how to do all the items and that you will use the results to teach them what they need to know. Try to make students feel that it is okay if they do not know how to do a section; they can skip it. If possible, you might consider communicating the purpose of the Inventory to older students through a bilingual student or parent.

Inventory Page 1

Name _____ Date _____

Language-Free Math Inventory
A. Count and Group Objects

_____

_____

_____

B. Count, Read and Write Numbers to 100

1, 2, 3, 4, 5, __6__, 7, 8, 9, 10, __11__, 12

45, 46, 47, 48, 49, 50, _____, 52, 53, _____, 55

89, 90, 91, 92, 93, _____, 95, 96, 97, 98, 99, _____

25, 26, 27, 28, 29, _____, 31, 32, 33, 34, 35, _____

Inventory Page 2

Name _____ Date _____

Language-Free Math Inventory

C. Compare Whole Numbers to 100

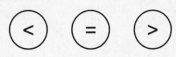

25 $\bigcirc$ 26   69 $\bigcirc$ 71   86 $\bigcirc$ 86

18 $\bigcirc$ 81   35 $\bigcirc$ 32   59 $\bigcirc$ 67

D. Count 2s, 5s, 10s, to a Hundred

2, 4, 6, __8__, 10

26, 28, 30, _____, 34

10, 12, 14, _____, _____

5, 10, 15, _____, 25

10, 20, 30, _____, _____

60, 70, _____, 90, _____

E. Number Sequencing

5
•

4•   •3   7•   •6

2•   •1   9•   •8
   16

15•   14 11   •10
       • •

13• •12

F. Add and Subtract Facts

−1		+1
4	5	6
	24	
	47	
	69	

−10		+10
50	60	70
	30	
	14	
	73	

Inventory Page 3

Name _____ Date _____

Language-Free Math Inventory

G. Addition and Subtraction Facts to 20

3 + 4	6 + 2	7 + 7	5 + 6	10 + 7	11 + 4	12 + 6

7

5 – 3	6 – 5	9 – 4	10 – 5	11 – 4	14 – 7	18 – 6

4 + 4 = _____   6 + 3 = _____   7 + 5 = _____   10 + 3 = _____

5 – 2 = _____   6 – 3 = _____   10 – 4 = _____   11 – 5 = _____

H. Add or Subtract Related Facts

5 + 3 = 8	16 – 7 = 9		2 + 2 = 4
6 + 6 = 12	8 – 5 = 3		3 – 2 = 1
9 + 7 = 16	15 – 12 = 3		5 – 3 = 2
12 + 3 = 15	12 – 6 = 6		1 + 2 = 3

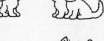 

I. Extended Patterns

1 2 1 2   1 2 1 ___ ___ ___ ___

Inventory Page 1

Name _____ Date _____

Language-Free Math Inventory
A. Count and Group Objects (Gr.1: NS 1.1)

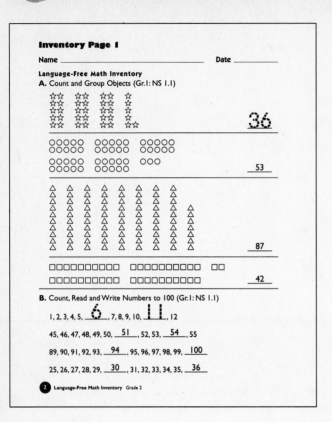

B. Count, Read and Write Numbers to 100 (Gr.1: NS 1.1)

1, 2, 3, 4, 5, **6**, 7, 8, 9, 10, **11**, 12

45, 46, 47, 48, 49, 50, **51**, 52, 53, **54**, 55

89, 90, 91, 92, 93, **94**, 95, 96, 97, 98, 99, **100**

25, 26, 27, 28, 29, **30**, 31, 32, 33, 34, 35, **36**

Inventory Page 2

Name _____ Date _____

Language-Free Math Inventory
C. Compare Whole Numbers to 100 (Gr.1: NS 1.2)

< = >

25 (<) 26   69 (<) 71   86 (=) 86

18 (<) 81   35 (>) 32   59 (<) 67

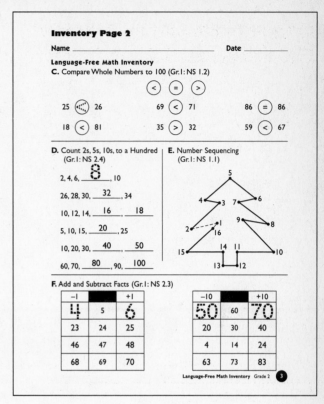

D. Count 2s, 5s, 10s, to a Hundred (Gr.1: NS 2.4)

2, 4, 6, **8**, 10

26, 28, 30, **32**, 34

10, 12, 14, **16**, **18**

5, 10, 15, **20**, 25

10, 20, 30, **40**, **50**

60, 70, **80**, 90, **100**

E. Number Sequencing (Gr.1: NS 1.1)

F. Add and Subtract Facts (Gr.1: NS 2.3)

–1		+1
4	5	**6**
23	24	25
46	47	48
68	69	70

–10		+10
50	60	**70**
20	30	40
4	14	24
63	73	83

Inventory Page 3

Name _____ Date _____

Language-Free Math Inventory
G. Addition and Subtraction Facts to 20 (Gr.1: NS 2.1)

3 + 4 **7**	6 + 2 8	7 + 7 14	5 + 6 11	10 + 7 17	11 + 4 15	12 + 6 18

5 – 3 2	6 – 5 1	9 – 4 5	10 – 5 5	11 – 4 7	14 – 7 7	18 – 6 12

4 + 4 = **8**   6 + 3 = **9**   7 + 5 = **12**   10 + 3 = **13**

5 – 2 = **3**   6 – 3 = **3**   10 – 4 = **6**   11 – 5 = **6**

H. Add or Subtract Related Facts (Gr.1: NS 2.2, 2.5)

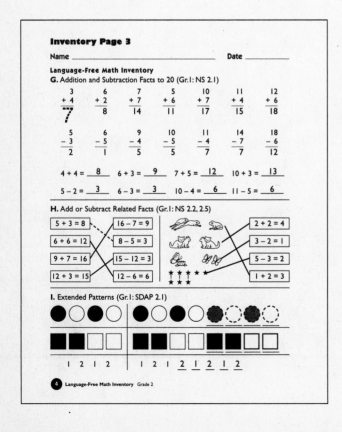

5 + 3 = 8   16 – 7 = 9   2 + 2 = 4
6 + 6 = 12   8 – 5 = 3   3 – 2 = 1
9 + 7 = 16   15 – 12 = 3   5 – 3 = 2
12 + 3 = 15   12 – 6 = 6   1 + 2 = 3

I. Extended Patterns (Gr.1: SDAP 2.1)

1 2 1 2   1 2 1 **2 1 2 1 2**

How to Use the Essential Math Vocabulary Inventory and Teaching Pages

The Essential Math Vocabulary section of the *English Language Learners Handbook* consists of an **Inventory** and **Teaching Pages**. The Inventory will help you to assess the skills that individual students have acquired to date. The Teaching Pages will give you strategies for developing specific math vocabulary.

The Inventory assesses acquisition of content vocabulary that students are typically expected to comprehend at the beginning of a given grade level. For example, a first-grade teacher expects a first grader to know what five means. In addition, directive language, such as *write, cut, circle, underline,* and *choose the correct answer,* is assessed.

The Teaching Pages offer suggestions for meeting students' needs based on their responses on the Inventory. Strategies for teaching the content vocabulary as well as the directive language are provided on these pages.

Administering the Inventory

Administer the Inventory to one student at a time. (If you must administer the Inventory to small groups rather than one on one, be aware that you will probably not be able to gather as much information about each student's skills. In this setting, students are more apt to influence each other.) Read each item aloud. To help students find the correct location of the item being assessed, either point to the line of instructions or use a flash card to show the specific item. (To create a set of flash cards, make an extra copy of the Inventory in advance, cut apart the sections, and glue each section to a card.) Allow students to work at their own pace. Try not to give hints. Be sure to date the first page of the Inventory for future reference.

Evaluating the Inventory

You have two options. You may wish to identify items that were not answered correctly and simply turn to the Teaching Pages for those items and apply the strategies. Your second option is to evaluate students' responses in a more detailed manner by checking if there is any part of the line of instructions that the student answered correctly. For example, in the line of instructions "Write the number five," is there anything that indicates an understanding of the word five? If *five* is indicated in some way, then the student understands the concept of five, but probably does not understand the directive, *write.* In this case, you would only have to teach the strategies for the directive language and not for the content vocabulary.

It is important to remember that repetition is the key to the success of a student acquiring a second language. It takes time to comprehend and remember the words. Therefore, it is suggested that you repeat the strategies as often as possible.

The construction of the sentences for students to repeat has purposely been kept simple so that syntax does not interfere with comprehension and recall. The multisensory approach of the student seeing the teacher show or do something, hearing the teacher use the vocabulary, and manipulating the materials through a concrete activity are intended to enhance memory.

It is suggested that you readminister the Inventory periodically to assess each student's progress

Inventory Page 1

Name _____ Date _____

Essential Math Vocabulary Inventory

Note to the Teacher: Read each item aloud. Allow ample time for completion. Each student will need crayons.

A 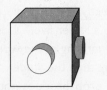 3

1. Circle the number.

2. Count how many. Write the number. _____

$$3 + 2 = 5$$

3. Color the picture for the addition sentence.

5   2+1=3

4. Circle the addition sentence.

---

3   **–**

$$4 - 1 = 3$$

5. Find the subtraction fact.

6. Color the clock red.

Inventory Page 2

Name _____   Date _____

Essential Math Vocabulary Inventory

Note to the Teacher: Read each item aloud. Allow ample time for completion. Each student will need crayons.

---

1. Use blue.
   Make a square.

   yes   no

2. Are these coins?
   Circle yes or no.

$1+2=3$

dog
cat
bird
fish

10

○   ○   ○   ○

3. Which shows a list?

4. Look at the figure.
   Mark its shape.

5. Look at the pictures.
   Color the one that shows time.

6. Find the price.
   Color it green.

Inventory Page 3

Name _____   Date _____

Essential Math Vocabulary Inventory

Note to the Teacher: Read each item aloud. Allow ample time for completion. Each student will need crayons, connecting cubes, pattern blocks, and counters.

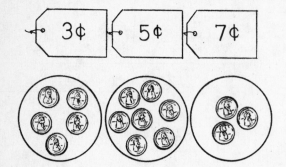

1. Match each group of coins to a price.

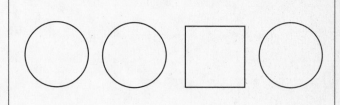

2. What doesn't belong? Mark an X on it.

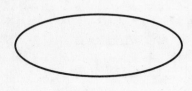

3. Trace a counter.

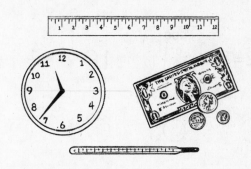

4. Look for the money. Color the correct picture.

5. Color the connecting cube yellow.

6. Circle the ruler with orange.

Inventory Page 4

Name _____ Date _____

Essential Math Vocabulary Inventory

Note to the Teacher: Read each item aloud. Allow ample time for completion. Each student will need crayons.

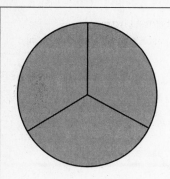

_____

1. How many parts?
   Write the number.

1   2   3   5

2. How many are left?
   Circle your answer.

1 + 1 =

1   2   3   4
○   ○   ○   ○

3. Choose the correct answer.

○ ○ ○ ○

4. Find the missing part.
   Fill in the bubble.

 ____ ____ ____

5. Count how many of each shape.
   Write the number.

---

1. Circle the number.

Materials
number cubes

Preparation
Write several X's on the board, making sure there is at least one X per child plus one for you.

DIRECTIVE LANGUAGE: CIRCLE

- Lead students in walking around the room. Walk in a circle around a few desks and chairs. Say: **Circle the desk. Circle the chair.** Then, lead students in walking to the chalkboard. Circle one of the X's on the board. Say: **Circle an X.** Let each student do the same at the board.

ESSENTIAL WORD: NUMBER

- Display 6 number cubes, each showing a different numeral from 1 to 6. Sequence the number cubes so that they are in numerical order. Say each number as you point to the cubes: **1, 2, 3, 4, 5, 6.**
- Lead students in placing counters next to each number cube to indicate the value of the numeral.
- Invite students to work in pairs to play Roll, Show, and Say. First, roll the number cube; then, use counters to show the number indicated; last, say the number. Offer students help as needed as they play.

---

2. Count how many. Write the number.

Materials
counters, number cube

DIRECTIVE LANGUAGE: COUNT HOW MANY

- Place 10 counters in a row, counting each one as you set it down. Count the counters again, touching each one as you say its number. Repeat several times, inviting students to join in.
- Take away some counters. Say: **Let's count how many** and then, do so. Repeat several times.
- Change the number of counters and repeat numerous times. Let volunteers lead the group in counting, too. Then, have students work in pairs to count objects around the room.

DIRECTIVE LANGUAGE: WRITE

- Refer to the directions for Roll, Show, and Say above. Modify the activity so that students roll the number cube and then, write the number. Encourage them to

say: **I can write the number _____ .**

ESSENTIAL WORD: NUMBER

- Refer to the directions under "Circle the number" for item 1 above.

---

3. Color the picture for the addition sentence.

Materials
old magazines, scissors, paste, crayons, sentence strips

Preparation
Write a variety of word sentences (for example, I can jump.) and addition sentences (for example, 2 + 3 = 5) on sentence strips.

Student will need:
old magazines, scissors, paste, crayons

ESSENTIAL WORD: PICTURE

- Display a magazine page with several pictures. As you point to each one, say: **This is a picture.**
- Cut out the pictures. Demonstrate how to paste them on paper to make a picture collage. Then, let students work in pairs to create their own picture collages.

DIRECTIVE LANGUAGE: COLOR THE PICTURE

- Demonstrate how to make a simple line drawing with a pencil. For example, you might make a simple animal. Then, demonstrate how to color the picture with crayons. Say: **I am going to color the picture.** Lead students in making and coloring their own pictures. Demonstrate again, as necessary.

ESSENTIAL WORDS: ADDITION SENTENCE

- Write these two sentences on the board, one above the other: I can jump. 2 + 3 = 5. Point to the first sentence and say: **This is a word sentence.** Point to the second sentence and say: **This is an addition sentence.**
- Place the sentence strips face down in a stack. Pick the first strip from the stack and show it to students. Ask: **Is it a word sentence or an addition sentence?** Say:

  Yes, it is a (an) _____ sentence.

- Let students take turns picking a strip and answering the question: **What kind of sentence is it?** Offer help as needed.

---

4. Circle the addition sentence.

Preparation
- Write several X's on the board, making sure there is at least one X per child plus one for you.

DIRECTIVE LANGUAGE: CIRCLE

- Refer to the directions under "Circle the number" for item 1 on page 12.

---

5. **Find the subtraction fact.**

   Materials
   pan of sand; small classroom items such as paper clips, pencils, and crayons; 20 index cards

   Preparation
   - Bury several small classroom items in a pan of sand. (If you want students to keep the items they find, bury items such as stickers or erasers.)
   - Write 10 basic subtraction facts vertically on index cards, one fact per card. Then, write the same facts horizontally on other cards.

DIRECTIVE LANGUAGE: FIND

- Demonstrate how to find something hidden in the sand. Ask: **What am I going to find?** Then, search for and find an item in the sand. Display it and say: **What did I find?** Then say: **I found a _____ .**
- Encourage students to search for items. Before each turn, lead the group in saying: **Find a _____** or **find a _____ .** Then ask: **What did you find?** Help students to use the prompt: **I found a _____ .**

ESSENTIAL WORDS: SUBTRACTION FACT

- Write a subtraction fact vertically on the board; below it write the same fact horizontally. Point to each fact and say: **This is a subtraction fact.**
- Then, display an index card with a vertical subtraction fact on it. Ask: **What is this?** and elicit that it is a subtraction fact. Repeat for a fact written horizontally.
- Mix up the 20 index cards and arrange them face down in 5 rows of 4. Demonstrate how to make a match by selecting 2 cards. Turn them over so everyone can see. Ask:

Are the subtraction facts the same? If they are, say: **These subtraction facts are the same.** Keep the match.
- Let play continue with a child picking 2 cards. If the cards do not match, say: **These subtraction facts are not the same.** Return them face down to their places.
- Let another child select the next 2 cards. Lead the group in determining if the facts are the same. Continue until all matches are made.

---

6. **Color the clock red.**

   Materials
   crayons, connecting cubes, demonstration clock

   Student will need:
   crayons

DIRECTIVE LANGUAGE: COLOR

- Display a box of crayons. Say: **We color with crayons.** Then, let students color pictures with the crayons.

ESSENTIAL WORD: RED

- Display connecting cubes. Pick up a red one and say: **It is red.** Pick up one that is another color and say: **It is not red,** shaking your head no as you say it.
- Repeat several times, letting students say whether or not the cube is red.
- Make a connecting cube tower from the red cubes you picked up. Let students make their own red cube towers.

ESSENTIAL WORD: CLOCK

- Point out the real clock in the classroom. Say: It is a clock. Point out the hands of the clock. Explain that a clock measures time.
- Display the demonstration clock. Say: This is a clock. Point out the hands. Lead students in saying the numbers around the clock face. Then, let students move the clock hands.

1. Use blue. Make a square.

Materials
crayons, connecting cubes, pattern blocks

Student will need:
crayons

If some students are not able to write their names . . .

Then, dot out each student's name and make a copy for each student to use for practice.

DIRECTIVE LANGUAGE: USE

- Demonstrate how to use a pencil to write your name. Say: **I use a pencil to write my name.** Have students do and say the same. Repeat using a crayon, and say: **I use a crayon to write my name.** Have students repeat.

ESSENTIAL WORD: BLUE

- Refer to the directions under "Color the clock red" for item 6 on page 00. Replace red with blue.

ESSENTIAL WORD: SQUARE

- Display pattern blocks. Pick up a square block and say: **This is a square.** Have students find more squares among the pattern blocks.
- Invite pairs of students to look for squares around the room. Encourage use of the word *square*.

DIRECTIVE LANGUAGE: MAKE A SQUARE

- Say: **I can make a square.** Then, demonstrate how to draw a square on paper. Invite students to do the same, while you say: **Make a square.**

2. Are these coins? Circle yes or no.

Materials
play coins, counters, pattern blocks, small chalkboard, paper cup

Preparation
If you decide to have students play store at this time, refer to Preparation under "Find the price. Color it green" for item 6 on page 15.

ESSENTIAL WORD: COINS

- Mix together and display play coins, counters, and pattern blocks. Find a penny, a nickel, a dime, and a quarter in the mixture. Say: **These are coins.** Let students find more coins in the mixture.
- You can extend the activity by having students sort the coins by kind (pennies, nickels, and so on). In addition, students can play store.

DIRECTIVE LANGUAGE: CIRCLE YES OR NO

- Write *yes* and *no* on the chalkboard. Ask students if your name is (say your name). Then say: **I am going to circle yes because my name is (say your name).** Erase the circle leaving yes and no on the board.
- Next, ask if your name is George Washington. Then say: **I am going to circle no because my name is not George Washington.**
- Extend the activity by playing a modified game of 20 Questions. Give a volunteer a paper cup to use to cover a small item. The student finds an item and shows it to the other students, but not to you. Then, ask the group yes/no questions about the item, such as **Is it green? Is it square?** and so on. Have the group figure out the answer. Let them take turns circling yes or no on the chalkboard. Continue until you guess the item or have asked 20 questions about it.

3. Which shows a list?

Preparation
Write a list of classroom items on paper. Include the following on the list: desk, chair, table, book, pencil, crayon.

ESSENTIAL WORD: LIST

- Display the list of classroom items. Match actual objects with the words on the list.
- Then, have students make a list of their names on the chalkboard.
- Refer to the directions below under "Look at the figure. Mark its shape" for those students who need help filling in the bubble.

4. Look at the figure. Mark its shape.

Materials
2 hand puppets, pattern blocks

Preparation
Write your name on the board along with three students' names. Write the names in a row.

Directive Language: LOOK AT THE FIGURE

- Have students watch a puppet show in which you make a simple figure with pattern blocks; for example, a house with a square and a triangle.
- Show the figure to two hand puppets, as you say: **Look at the figure.** Have one puppet look at the figure and the other puppet look elsewhere. Say things like: **You are *not* looking at the figure** to the inattentive puppet and **What do you see when you look at the figure?** to the attentive puppet, who answers, **I see a house.**
- Ask students to look at the figure again. Then, invite students to replicate the figure with pattern blocks.

Directive Language: MARK

- Draw a bubble below each name on the chalkboard as you read it aloud. Ask students which name is yours. Help them find your name. Then say: **I am going to mark my name,** as you fill in the bubble.

Essential Word: SHAPE

- Display pattern blocks. Say: **These have many shapes.** Name the different shapes.
- Invite students to sort the blocks by shape (if the group is large, divide students and blocks into smaller groups).
- Next, have pairs of students select two shapes and make figures. Encourage use of the word shape as students create their figures.

---

5. Look at the pictures. Color the one that shows time.

Materials
poster or magazine picture (see Preparation), crayons, clock

Preparation
If you do not have an appropriate poster, find a magazine picture with enough detail for students to distinguish different items. Select as large a picture as possible for easy viewing.

Student will need:
crayons

Directive Language: LOOK AT THE PICTURES

- Show students a poster or an interesting picture cut from a magazine. Say: **Look at the picture.**
- Ask questions that allow students to point out parts of the picture or to describe details, based on students' language acquisition levels. For example, **Where is the dog?** allows a gestured answer; however, **What is the dog doing?** requires an explanation.

Directive Language: COLOR

- Refer to the directions under "Color the clock red" for item 6 on page 13.

Essential Word: TIME

- Ask students to sit without moving or talking for one minute. Use the movements of the minute hand on a clock to keep track of the time. Make sure students see you using the clock.
- When the time is up, explain that one minute of time has passed. Invite students to describe their experience (many will think it was a long time). Compare different times, such as how long recess is, how long the school day is, and how long a favorite program is.

---

6. Find the price. Color it green.

Materials
pan of sand; small classroom items such as paper clips, pencils, and crayons; other small classroom items and toys, such as pencils, erasers, toy cups, and toy cars; masking tape; play coins; toy cash register (optional); crayons; connecting cubes

Preparation
- Bury several small classroom items in a pan of sand.
- Mark other small classroom items and toys with simple price tags (masking tape squares) marked in cents (for example, a pencil for 5¢).

Student will need:
crayons

Directive Language: FIND

- Refer to the directions under "Find the subtraction fact" for item 5 on page 13.

Essential Word: PRICE

- Show students several items with simple price tags marked in cents. Point out a price tag and say: **This is the price.** Have students find the price on the other items.
- Let students play store by interacting with the priced items and play coins. If a toy cash register is available, let them use it, too. Allow free exploration. Leave store items in a center for students to use at other times.

Directive Language: COLOR

- Refer to the directions under "Color the clock red" for item 6 on page 13.

Essential Word: GREEN

- Refer to the directions under "Color the clock red" for item 6 on page 13. Replace red with green.

---

1. Match each group of coins to a price.

Materials
pattern blocks, crayons, unit cubes, connecting cubes, counters, play coins

Preparation
See Preparation for the play store on page 14.

DIRECTIVE LANGUAGE: MATCH

- Display pattern blocks. Make a row composed of pattern blocks in every color. Say: **I am going to match colors.**
- Find a blue pattern block and place it below the blue block in the row. Repeat for yellow. Let students match the remaining blocks.
- Extend by matching crayons to the colors of the blocks.

ESSENTIAL WORD: GROUP

- Display unit cubes, connecting cubes, counters, and pattern blocks all mixed together. Say: **I am going to make a group.**
- Find 5 counters and put them together. Say: **I am going to make another group,** and do so with connecting cubes.
- Let students make groups. Say: **Make a group.** Model saying: **I have a group.** Have students repeat. Invite students to make several more groups.

ESSENTIAL WORD: COINS

- Refer to the directions under "Are these coins? Circle yes or no" for item 2 on page 14.

ESSENTIAL WORD: PRICE

- Refer to the directions under "Find the price. Color it green" for item 6 on page 15.

---

2. What doesn't belong? Mark an X on it.

Materials
pattern blocks; real objects such as 3 shoes and a stapler, 5 paper clips and an eraser, 4 books and a box of crayons; beanbags

---

ESSENTIAL WORDS: WHAT DOESN'T BELONG

- Show a row of 5 red pattern blocks and 1 yellow one in the middle. Point to the yellow block and say: **This one doesn't belong.** Replace the yellow one with a blue one. Ask: **What doesn't belong?** Depending on stu-

dents' language-acquisition levels, you may wish to discuss why the yellow one didn't belong and why the blue one doesn't.
- Let volunteers make rows of one color with an additional block of another color. Have them ask the group: **What doesn't belong?** You can extend the activity by using real objects, such as 3 shoes and a stapler; 5 paper clips and an eraser; and 4 books and a box of crayons.

DIRECTIVE LANGUAGE: MARK AN X ON IT

- Demonstrate how to play beanbag toss by throwing a beanbag at a sheet of paper on the floor. Say: **I am going to mark an X on it.** Then, mark an X on the paper to show where the beanbag landed. Repeat several times, marking an X only when the beanbag actually lands on the paper. Let students play Beanbag Toss and mark an X on the paper where the beanbag lands.

---

3. Trace a counter.

Materials
pattern blocks, counters

DIRECTIVE LANGUAGE: TRACE

- Demonstrate how to trace around pattern blocks. Say: **I trace around it.** Then, have students make simple pictures with pattern blocks and trace around them to record their drawings.

ESSENTIAL WORD: COUNTER

- Display a counter and say: **This is a counter.** Demonstrate how to line up a handful of counters and count them. Let students work in pairs taking turns grabbing a handful and lining them up.
- Then, have partners work together to count the counters. Offer counting help as needed.

---

4. Look for the money. Color the correct picture.

Materials
classroom items such as scissors; play money; large sheet of paper; crayons

Preparation
Make simple outline drawings of a ball, a stick person, a cup, and an apple on a large sheet of paper.

Student will need:
crayons

DIRECTIVE LANGUAGE: LOOK FOR

- Demonstrate how to play with an English-proficient student. Show everyone a pair of scissors. Say: **Look for scissors.** The child helping you then looks for a pair of scissors and shows it to everyone. Have students look for a variety of items; give visual examples to support your directions.

ESSENTIAL WORD: MONEY

- Refer to the directions under "Are these coins? Circle yes or no" for item 2 on page 14. Include play dollar bills in the activity.

DIRECTIVE LANGUAGE: COLOR THE CORRECT PICTURE

- Focus attention on the simple drawings on the large sheet of paper. Name each item.
- Ask students to look for the ball. After they have identified the ball, say: **I am going to color the correct picture,** and do so.
- Let each child draw four items in pencil on paper. Have students form pairs and exchange papers. Have each partner choose a pictured item for the other person to color. Say: **Color the correct picture.**

---

5. Color the connecting cube yellow.

Materials
crayons, connecting cubes

Student will need:
crayons, connecting cubes

DIRECTIVE LANGUAGE: COLOR

- Refer to the directions under "Color the clock red" for item 6 on page 13.

ESSENTIAL WORDS: CONNECTING CUBE

- Display connecting cubes. Say: **These are connecting cubes.** Demonstrate how to make a tower, a train, and a larger cube with the connecting cubes.
- Have students work in pairs to build with the cubes. Encourage students to use vocabulary as they share the cubes.

ESSENTIAL WORD: YELLOW

- Refer to the directions under "Color the clock red" for item 6 on page 13. Replace red with yellow.

---

6. Circle the ruler with orange.

Materials
ruler, crayons, connecting cubes

Student will need:
ruler, crayons

DIRECTIVE LANGUAGE: CIRCLE

- Refer to the directions under "Circle the number" for item 1 on page 12.

ESSENTIAL WORD: RULER

- Display a ruler. Say: **This is a ruler.** Have students repeat. Demonstrate how to use the ruler to draw straight lines. Then, let students create their own line art by drawing a variety of colored lines with crayon and a ruler.

ESSENTIAL WORD: ORANGE

- Refer to the directions under "Color the clock red" for item 6 on page 00. Replace red with orange.

1. How many parts? Write the number.

Materials
number cubes, counters, toy car that can be taken apart

DIRECTIVE LANGUAGE: WRITE THE NUMBER

- Refer to the directions under "Count how many. Write the number" for item 2 on page 12.

ESSENTIAL WORDS: HOW MANY

- Display a row of counters. Ask: **How many?** Then, lead students in counting. Repeat with different amounts of counters.
- Let students form pairs and count various objects in the room, such as books on a bookshelf, crayons in a box, paper clips in a cup, and so on. Encourage students to ask and answer the question: **How many?**

ESSENTIAL WORD: PARTS

- Display a toy car. Take it apart and point to the parts. Say: **These are the parts of the car.** Invite volunteers to put the parts back together to make the whole car.

2. How many are left? Circle your answer.

Materials
counters

ESSENTIAL WORDS: HOW MANY ARE LEFT

- Display 6 counters, and count them aloud with students. Let students see you remove 2 of the counters. Ask: **How many are left?** Count the remaining counters with students. Repeat several times varying the number of counters.
- Give pairs of students a handful of counters. Let each pair count the counters, remove some, and count again to answer: **How many are left?**

DIRECTIVE LANGUAGE: CIRCLE YOUR ANSWER

- Continue with the preceding activity; however, this time, write the numbers from 1 through 10 on the board. When students determine how many are left, model how to circle the answer. Say: **I am going to circle your answer,** and then do so. Once students catch on, let them circle the answer for future rounds.

3. Choose the correct answer.

Materials
spinner, counters

If students need additional practice reading numerals and counting . . .

Then, play a game in which students spin spinners with numerals from 7-20, show the numbers with counters and then, say the numbers.

DIRECTIVE LANGUAGE: CHOOSE THE CORRECT ANSWER

- Display rows of counters to match the numbers on a spinner. For example, if the spinner has 1, 2, 3, 4 on it, you would need rows with 1, 2, 3, and 4 counters.
- Spin a spinner as students observe. Have students read the number. Say: **I am going to choose the correct answer.** Point to the row of counters that matches the spinner. Let students take turns spinning the spinner.
  Each time, say: **Choose the correct answer.**
- Refer to the directions under "Look at the figure. Mark its shape" for item 4 on page 15 for those students who need help filling in the bubble.

4. Find the missing part. Fill in the bubble.

Materials
puzzle, old magazines, scissors

Preparation
Cut out pictures of objects from magazines. After cutting out each object, cut off part of it to make a missing part. Save all parts for students to match up later.

DIRECTIVE LANGUAGE: FILL IN THE BUBBLE

- Refer to the directions under "Look at the figure. Mark its shape" for item 4 on page 15. Say: **I am going to fill in the bubble,** as you mark the bubble.

ESSENTIAL WORDS: FIND THE MISSING PART

- Remove one piece of a puzzle. Show the incomplete puzzle to students. Say: **I am going to find the missing part.** Look for the missing part among other parts of toys, such as wheels or a doll's shoe.
- Display the magazine pictures with missing parts. Have students find the missing parts.

5. Use the picture. Count how many of each shape. Write the number.

Materials
pattern blocks, counters, number cubes

Preparation
Prepare the following collection of pattern blocks and counters: 3 triangles, 4 squares, 2 rectangles, 6 circles. For each pair of students, make a different collection with up to 10 blocks or counters of any given shape.

ESSENTIAL WORD: SHAPE

- Display pattern blocks and counters. Trace your finger around the different shapes. Say: **This shape is**

  a _____ , filling in the blank with the correct shape name. Let students make pattern block pictures using the different shapes.

DIRECTIVE LANGUAGE: COUNT HOW MANY OF EACH SHAPE

- Display the following collection of pattern blocks and counters: 3 triangles, 4 squares, 2 rectangles, 6 circles. Then say: **Let's count how many of each shape.** Lead students in doing so. Repeat the statement several times.
- Have students work in pairs. Give each pair a different collection of pattern blocks and counters to count.

DIRECTIVE LANGUAGE: WRITE THE NUMBER

- Refer to the directions under "Count how many. Write the number" for item 2 on page 12.

PAGE 1

1. "3" circled
2. "4" written
3. picture at left colored
4. "2 + 1 = 3" circled
5. "4 - 1 = 3" circled
6. clock colored red

PAGE 2

1. blue square drawn in space
2. "yes" circled
3. bubble below list filled in
4. triangle filled in
5. picture at right showing clock colored
6. price tag colored green

PAGE 3

1. line drawn from 3¢ to group with 3 pennies, from 5¢ to group with 5 pennies, from 7¢ to group with 7 pennies
2. X marked through square
3. counter outline in space to show student traced the shape
4. dollar bill with coins colored
5. connecting cube colored yellow
6. ruler circled orange

PAGE 4

1. "3" written
2. "2" circled
3. bubble next to "2" filled in
4. bubble below shoe filled in
5. "2" written beside (square), "1" written beside (circle), "3" written beside (rectangle)

CHAPTER 1 Addition and Subtraction Strategies and Facts to 12

CLUSTER A, PAGES 1-12

Objectives

- use a number line to add on 0, 1, 2, or 3
- change the order of addends and add
- set a purpose for reading

Cluster A Materials

- 2-color counters
- crayons
- index cards
- masking tape
- Activity Page 1-A

Math Words

Words	Examples
add	Combine a group of 7 connecting cubes and 5 connecting cubes to demonstrate 7 + 3 = 10.
addend	7 + 3 = 10
count on	Using a number line, start on 7 and say 8, 9, 10 to model 7 + 3 = 10.
number line	Show an example of a number line and use it to demonstrate counting on.
sum	7 + 3 = 10
turnaround facts	7 + 3 = 10 3 + 7 = 10

Teaching Strategies See pp. v–vi for teaching tips on working with ELL students.

1•1 ADDITION STRATEGIES

Materials: masking tape, index cards

- Write addition facts such as 4 + 0, 5 + 2, 8 + 1, and 9 + 3 on index cards. Use masking tape to make a number line from 0–12 across the floor. Have students say the numbers as you write them.
- Have a volunteer pick a card, for example, 5 + 2. Ask the student to stand on 5 on the number line and jump ahead 2 numbers, saying 5, 6, 7. Explain that the volunteer just used a number line to *count on*. Have students say *5 plus 2 equals 7* as you write the completed fact on the chalkboard.

- Follow the same procedure with other volunteers and facts. (Save the number line for Activity 1•5.)

1•2 TURNAROUND FACTS

Materials: red and yellow crayons, Activity Page 1-A

- Distribute crayons and an activity page to each student. Have students point to the first blank domino in row 1. Ask them to make 4 red dots on the left side and 3 yellow dots on the right side. Ask how many dots they made in all. Have students write 4 + 3 = 7 below the domino. Explain that 4 and 3 are called addends and that 7 is the sum. Write the words on the chalkboard, and have students read them aloud with you.
- Point to the second domino in row 1. Instruct students as follows:
- **Draw 3 yellow dots on the left side; draw 4 red dots on the right side; write 3 + 4 = 7 below the domino.**
- Focus attention on the 2 facts below the dominos. **How are the 2 facts alike and different?** *They use the same numbers, but they're in a different order; the sums are the same.* Explain that these facts are called turnaround facts because the sums do not change when you turn around the addends.
- Have students complete the page by illustrating and writing turnaround facts for 2 and 6, 5 and 4, 8 and 2, and 9 and 3.

1•3 READING FOR MATH • READ TO SET A PURPOSE

Materials: 2-color counters

- Draw a simple picture with these elements: a stick figure of a girl, a flowerpot with 5 red tulips, and one with 6 red tulips. Write the following story on the chalkboard and read it with students: **Flora Fern likes flowers. Flora has 5 red flowers in one pot. She has 6 yellow flowers in another pot.**
- Have students look at the picture and reread story. **What information does the story give you?** *how many red and yellow flowers Flora has* Call on volunteers to underline the information. **How many red flowers does Flora have?** *5* **How many yellow flowers does she have?** *6* **How many flowers does Flora have in all?** *11* Call on a volunteer to write a number sentence that shows how many flowers Flora has. *6 + 5 = 11* Have students make a model of the sentence with counters.
- Remind students that as they read a story problem, they should look for the important information that will help them to solve it.

Activity Page 1-A

Name _____ Date _____

Exploring Turnaround Facts

Show and write turnaround facts.

Listen to your teacher's directions.

1.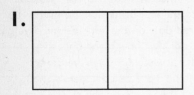

_____ + _____ = _____   _____ + _____ = _____

2.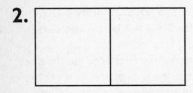

_____ + _____ = _____   _____ + _____ = _____

3.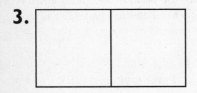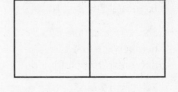

_____ + _____ = _____   _____ + _____ = _____

4.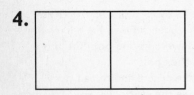

_____ + _____ = _____   _____ + _____ = _____

5.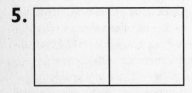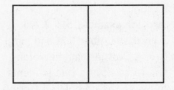

_____ + _____ = _____   _____ + _____ = _____

Objectives

- draw a picture to solve a problem
- count back to subtract
- use addition facts to subtract
- complete fact families

Cluster B Materials

- counters
- crayons
- index cards
- number line
- picture of ladybug
- Activity Page 1-B

Math Words

Words	Examples
count back	Using a number line, start on 10 and say 9, 8, 7 to show $10 - 3 = 7$.
difference	$10 - 3 = 7$
fact family	$7 + 3 = 10$ $10 - 3 = 7$ $3 + 7 = 10$ $10 - 7 = 3$
related facts	$7 + 3 = 10$ $10 - 3 = 7$
subtract	$7 + 3 = 10$
turnaround facts	Show a connecting-cube train of 7 red and 3 blue cubes and then snap off 3 cubes to show $10 - 3 = 7$.

Teaching Strategies See pp. v–vi for teaching tips on working with ELL students.

1•4 PROBLEM SOLVING STRATEGY • DRAW A PICTURE

Materials: crayons, picture of ladybug, counters (optional), Activity Page 1-B

- Write this story problem on 3 lines on the chalkboard: **There are 5 ladybugs on the plant. 4 more ladybugs land on the plant. How many ladybugs are there in all?** Display a picture of a ladybug and read the story aloud with students.
- **What do you know?** *5 ladybugs are on the plant, 4 more land on the plant.* **What do you want to find out?** *how many ladybugs there are in all* Suggest that students draw a picture to help them solve the problem.
- Distribute activity pages and crayons to students. Reread the first line of the problem. **How many ladybugs will you draw on the plant?** *5* Reread the second line of the problem. **How many more ladybugs**

will you draw on the plant? *4* Have students draw the ladybugs and then tell how many there are in all. *9*
- Have students write an addition sentence to tell about their drawing. *5 + 4 = 9* NOTE: You may wish to have students first solve several ladybug problems by placing counters on the plant leaves to represent the ladybugs and then have them draw a picture to show one of the problems they solved.

1•5 COUNT BACK TO SUBTRACT

Materials: number line from Activity 1•1, index cards
- Write subtraction facts such as $7 - 2$, $11 - 3$, $12 - 2$, $9 - 1$; $4 - 0$ on index cards.
- Have a volunteer pick a card, for example, $7 - 2$. Ask the student to stand on 7 on the number line and jump back 2 numbers, saying 7, 6, 5. Explain that he or she just used a number line to *count back*. Have the student say *7 minus 2 equals 5* as you write the completed fact on the chalkboard.
- Follow the same procedure with other volunteers.

1•6 RELATE ADDITION AND SUBTRACTION

Materials: red and blue connecting cubes
- Have students work in pairs. Distribute red cubes to one partner and blue cubes to the other.
- Have one partner connect 5 red cubes. Have the other partner connect 4 blue cubes. Then, have partners connect the 2 groups of cubes to make a cube train. Have partners say and then write an addition fact to show what they did. *5 + 4 = 9*
- Have one partner remove the 4 blue cubes. Have partners then say and write a subtraction fact to show what they did. *9 - 4 = 5* Tell students that they just demonstrated and wrote 2 related facts. **Why do you think they are called related facts?** *They have the same numbers.*
- Have students follow the same procedure with other related facts.

1•7 FACT FAMILIES

Materials: 5 index cards per student, crayons
- Assign each student a different pair of numbers such as 2 and 4 or 9 and 3, which when added have a sum of 12 or less. Have students fold 1 index card in half, hold it horizontally, and draw dots on the left side and the right to represent the 2 numbers. **How many dots are on the left? How many are on the right? How many dots are there in all?** Have students write the addition fact (for example, $2 + 4 = 6$) on a second card.
- Then, have students turn their dot cards around and write the turnaround fact (for example, $4 + 2 = 6$) on a third index card.

- Next, ask students to hold their dot cards vertically. **How many dots do you have in all?** Have students fold the top half back so that only the dots on the bottom half are visible. **How many dots are left?** Have students write a subtraction fact, for example, 6 – 4 = 2, on a fourth card. Have students then turn the dot card again and write the new subtraction fact (for example, 6 – 2 = 4) on the last card.

- Explain that the 4 facts students wrote belong to the same *fact family*. Invite students to tell about their fact family to a partner and then trade cards. Have them use their dot cards to explain the fact cards.

Activity Page 1-B

Name _____   Date _____

Drawing a Picture to Solve a Problem

Read the problem.

Draw the ladybugs on the plant.

Draw the ladybugs that land on the plant.

Write a number sentence to tell about your picture.

Then color the picture.

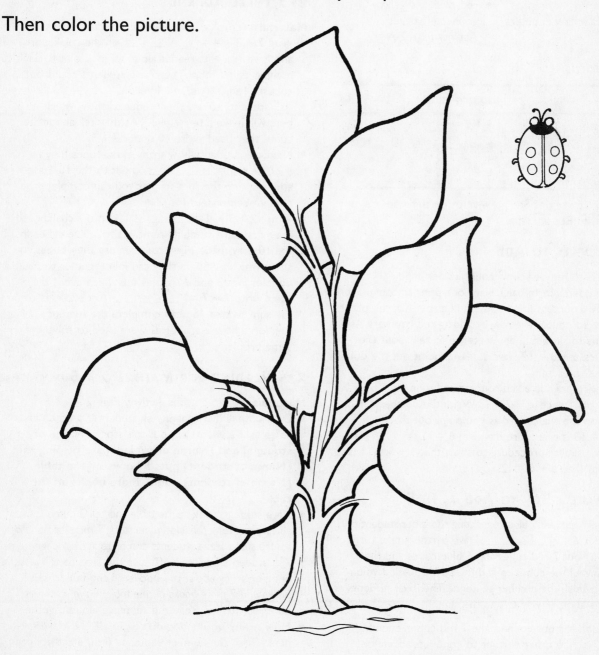

CHAPTER 2 Addition and Subtraction Strategies and Facts to 20

CLUSTER A, PAGES 37-50

Objectives

- use doubles to add
- make a ten to add 7, 8, 9
- add 3 numbers by using doubles and making tens
- use a short way to summarize a story problem

Cluster A Materials

- crayons
- red and yellow counters
- red, blue, and yellow connecting cubes
- Activity Page 2-A

Math Words

Words	Examples
doubles	7 + 7 = 14
	to show 10 − 3 = 7.
sum	8 + 7 = 15

Teaching Strategies See pp. v–vi for teaching tips on working with ELL students.

2•1 DOUBLES TO ADD

Materials: 10 red or yellow counters per child
- Have students form pairs. Have one partner count out 6 yellow counters and put them in a row. Ask the other partner to double the row by adding red counters. Ask students to say a number sentence to tell about the counters. *6 + 6 = 12* Have students point out the doubles and the sum.
- Have partners add a red counter and then say a new number sentence. *6 + 7 = 13* Write the number sentence on the chalkboard as you point out that 6 + 7 = 13 is one more than 6 + 6 = 12.
- Follow a similar procedure to show that 6 + 5 = 11 is one less than 6 + 6 = 12.

2•2 MAKE A TEN TO ADD 7, 8, 9

Materials: 9 red and 9 blue connecting cubes per student pair
- Write 7 + 6 = _____. Have partners take turns counting out 7 red cubes and 6 blue cubes and then counting all the cubes to find the sum. *13* Ask a volunteer to finish the number sentence. Then, tell students there is another way to find the sum.
- Have one partner connect the 7 red cubes, counting aloud. Ask the other partner to continue, adding on blue cubes until there are 10. Tell partners they have just made a ten. Write 10 on the chalkboard. **How many extras are there?** *3* Complete the number sentence on the chalkboard: 10 + 3 = _____. Have partners find the sum. *13* Ask a volunteer to complete the number sentence.
- Point to both number sentences. **What do you know about 7 + 6 and 10 + 3?** *The sums are the same.* Repeat with other problems to add 7, 8, and 9.

2•3 THREE ADDENDS

Materials: red, blue, and yellow connecting cubes
- Write 7 + 3 + 4 = _____ on the chalkboard and have students read it aloud as you point to each number and symbol. Then, have students count out cubes: 7 red, 3 blue, and 4 yellow.
- Ask students to use their cubes to show which numbers will make a ten. *7 and 3* As they tell about the cubes they used, write 10 under 7 + 3.
- Next, ask students how many extra cubes they have. *4* Write + 4 = _____ next to the 10. Have students find the sum so that you can complete the number sentence. *14*
- Write 7 + 3 + 4 = _____ on the chalkboard again and have students remove the 3 blue cubes from the 10 they made. Have students use their cubes to show which numbers they can join together to make a doubles fact. *3 and 4* As they tell which cubes they used, write 7 + 7 = _____. Ask students to find the sum so that you can complete the sentence. *14* Reinforce how 2 strategies were used to solve the same problem.

2•4 READING FOR MATH: DO A SUMMARY

Materials: books, crayons, Activity Page 2-A
- Distribute activity pages. Ask students to watch and listen as 2 students act out this story: **[Name of student] and [Name of student] are helping me. [Name of student] puts 5 books on the table. [Name of student] puts 7 more books on the table.**
- Have students look at the table and tell 2 number facts about the story. *5 books in one stack, 7 more books in a second stack.* Have students complete activity page item 1.
- Ask students how they can use the facts to tell a short number story about the books on the table. *I see 5 books and 7 more books on the table.* Have students complete item 2. Read the sentence aloud together.
- **How many books do you see in all?** *12.* Have students finish the number sentence on the activity page.

Activity Page 2-A

Name _____   Date _____

Summarizing the Facts of a Story

Listen as your teacher tells a story problem. Then follow the directions.

1. What number facts do you know? For each fact, write a number on the line and draw a picture.

_____   _____

2. Finish the sentence to tell the number story.

   I see _____ books and _____ more
   books on the table.

3. How many books do you see in all?
   Finish the number sentence.

   _____ + _____ = _____

Objectives

- write a number sentence
- use doubles facts to subtract
- relate addition and subtraction
- find missing addends
- use related addition and subtraction facts to make fact families
- practice making decisions

Cluster B Materials

- blue and yellow connecting cubes
- blue and yellow crayons
- index cards
- large paper circles
- sentence strips
- small self-stick notes
- Activity Page 2-B

Math Words

Words	Examples	
difference	$16 - 8 = 8$	
fact family	$8 + 7 = 15$	$15 - 7 = 8$
	$7 + 8 = 15$	$15 - 8 = 7$

Teaching Strategies See pp. v–vi for teaching tips on working with ELL students.

2•5 PROBLEM SOLVING: WRITE A NUMBER SENTENCE

Materials: per student pair: blue and yellow connecting cubes, blue and yellow crayons, Activity Page 2-B

- First, have one partner connect some blue cubes. Then, have the other partner add some yellow cubes. Next, have both partners draw and color on the worksheet the cubes they joined.
- **How many blue cubes did you use? How many yellow cubes? Will you add or subtract to find how many cubes you used in all? Why?** *Add, because cubes were joined together* Have partners complete item 2.
- Now, ask partners to remove some cubes. To complete items 3 and 4 on the worksheet, instruct partners to make an x on each cube they removed and then complete the number sentence. Offer prompts as needed. Invite pairs of students to share their work.

2•6 DOUBLES TO SUBTRACT

Materials: connecting cubes of 2 colors, 10 per color

- Have students form pairs. Ask one partner to say and show a doubles fact such as $6 + 6 = 12$ using cubes of 2 colors.

- Have the other partner remove all the cubes of one color and say a subtraction sentence to tell how many are left.
- Have the partners write the 2 number sentences.
- Next, ask students to look at the addends in the addition sentence and the difference in the subtraction sentence. **What do you notice?** *The numbers are the same.*

2•7 RELATE ADDITION AND SUBTRACTION

Materials: 17 large paper circles numbered from 1–17 taped in order across the floor

- Ask a student to stand on the 9, hop ahead 4 spaces, and call out the number on the circle. *13* Write $9 + 4 = 13$ on the chalkboard.
- Next, have the student turn around, hop back 4 spaces, and call out the number on the circle. *9* Write $13 - 4 = 9$ on the chalkboard and talk about how the 2 facts are related.
- Continue by having students generate other related addition and subtraction facts.

2•8 MISSING ADDENDS

Materials: related addition and subtraction number sentences on sentence strips, self-stick notes, connecting cubes of 2 colors

- Give partners a pair of related facts, such as $7 + 8 = 15$ and $15 - 7 = 8$, and connecting cubes of 2 colors. Have one partner read the addition fact and use the cubes to show it. Have the other partner read the subtraction fact and use the same cubes to show it.
- Use a self-stick note to cover the addend that is the same as the difference. Challenge partners to identify the missing number. They can remove the self-stick note to check.

2•9 FACT FAMILIES

Materials: related addition and subtraction fact cards to 20 with sums and differences omitted

- Give each student a fact card to complete. Then have students form a circle. Ask one student to stand in the circle and say the fact as the others check their cards. Explain that if all 3 numbers are the same, they may join the student in the circle because they are members of the same fact family. Encourage each "family member" to read his or her fact card aloud.
- Continue until all fact families are identified.

Activity Page 2-B

Name _____ Date _____

Writing Number Sentences to Tell About a Picture

1. Take turns with a partner. Put some cubes together.
Draw and color the cubes you put together.

2. Fill in the number sentence to tell about the cubes.

_____ ☐ _____ = _____

3. Now take away some cubes from the picture above.
Make an X on each cube to show this.

4. Fill in the number sentence.

_____ ☐ _____ = _____

CHAPTER 3　Place Value

Objectives

- make groups of ten
- estimate the number of objects in a group
- identify the tens and ones in 2-digit numbers
- read and write numbers to 99 as words
- understand and write 2-digit numbers in expanded form
- use clues to draw conclusions

Cluster A Materials

- connecting cubes
- counters
- crayons
- elastic bands
- large index cards
- number cards
- number-word cards
- paper bags
- plastic straws
- Activity Page 3-A

Math Words

Words	Examples
digit	23 ↓ ↓ means　means 2 tens　3 ones
estimate	about 10 ○○○○○ ○○○○○
expanded form	53 = 50 + 3
ones	25
regroup	23 ones = 2 tens 3 ones
tens	25

Teaching Strategies See pp. v–vi for teaching tips on working with ELL students.

3•1 TENS

Materials: connecting cubes; number cards 10, 20, 30, 40, 50

- Display the number cards on the chalkboard ledge and have students say each number as you point to it.
- Give each student 10, 20, 30, 40, or 50 cubes to make into groups of 10. Call on each student to tell how many tens he or she has and then hold up the correct number card on the ledge, saying how many in all. For

example, *I have 3 tens or 30 in all* Reinforce the concept that 10 ones make 1 ten or 10 in all, 20 ones make 2 tens or 20 in all, and so on.

3•2 MORE TENS

Materials: connecting cubes or counters, 10 per student; paper bags with 11, 19, 28, 36, or 48 cubes or counters; index cards labeled *about 10, about 20, about 30, about 40, about 50*

- Display the cards on the chalkboard ledge. Give partners 10 cubes or counters. Have partners count the cubes and set them aside in a pile.
- Give partners a bag of cubes. Have them empty the bag but not count the cubes. Have partners then tell about how many cubes were in the bag using their pile of 10 cubes to help. When partners think they know, have them take a card and say, for example, *We have about 20 cubes.* Finally, partners can count the cubes to check their estimates.

3•3 TENS AND ONES

Materials: 11–49 plastic straws or connecting cubes per student, elastic bands

- Distribute enough sticks so that students have ones left over when they make tens. Explain that each straw stands for a 1. Have students count their straws and tell how many ones they have.
- Have students regroup the ones by making bundles of 10, then tell how many tens and ones they have; for example, 3 tens and 2 ones. Record their responses as 2-digit numbers.

3•4 NUMBERS TO 100

Materials: number cards for 1–100, number-word cards from 1 to 100

- Have small groups of students form 2 lines. Give a number card to each student in one line and a corresponding word card to each student in the other line.
- At your signal, have students hold up their cards, look for someone with the matching word or number, and then stand together. Have partners read aloud and display their cards.

3•5 EXPANDED FORM

Materials: crayons, connecting cubes, Activity Page 3-A

- Have students pick a number between 11 and 49, such as 29. Write the number on the chalkboard. Have students use cubes to show the number in tens and ones.

Draw a picture on the chalkboard to demonstrate what students show. Then, ask students to tell how many tens and ones they have as you write the information on the chalkboard: 2 tens 9 ones.

- Tell students that there is another way to write 29. Write 20 + 9 and "expanded form" on the chalkboard. Ask students to read the words. Then point to each digit in turn and ask what it means. *20; 9 ones or 9*
- Distribute the activity page. Have students pick a new number and follow the directions to complete the page.

3•6 READING FOR MATH: DRAW CONCLUSIONS

- Have volunteers pretend as follows: 4 pretend to be having fun as they play a game; 7 pretend to be working

and not having fun. Ask students to watch and listen as you tell a story: **Some friends finished their work. They are playing a game. Some friends are still working.**
- **Are more children working or playing?** *working* **How many more?** *3 more* **How can you tell?** *by subtracting 7 – 4* **Which group do you think is having a better time?** *the children playing a game* **Why?** *They are smiling.* Explain that conclusions can be drawn by putting clues together.

Activity Page 3-A

Name _____ Date _____

Writing a Number as Tens and Ones

1. Write a number between 11 and 49. _____

2. Use connecting cubes.
   Show how many tens and ones.

3. Draw the cubes below. Write how many tens and ones.

_____ Tens   _____ Ones

4. Now write your number in expanded form.

   _____

Objectives

- use logical reasoning to solve problems
- use >, <, and = to compare numbers
- order numbers that come before, after, and between other numbers
- skip count by twos, threes, fours, and fives
- identify even and odd numbers
- use ordinal numbers from first through twelfth

Cluster B Materials

- counters
- crayons
- number cards
- number line
- sentence strips
- tens rods
- unit cubes
- Activity Page 3-B

Math Words

Words	Examples
after	48 comes **after** 47
before	46 comes **before** 47
between	47 comes **between** 46 and 48
compare	22 < 35, 35 > 22, 22 = 22
counting pattern	3 6 9 12 15 18
even	2 4 8 14 20 30 36
is equal to	22 = 22
is greater than	35 > 22
is less than	22 < 35
odd	1 3 5 7 15 19 31 45
order	1 2 3 4 5 6 7 8
ordinal number	first, second, third, fourth
skip count	2 4 6 8 10 12 14 16

Teaching Strategies See pp. v–vi for teaching tips on working with ELL students.

3•7 PROBLEM SOLVING: USE LOGICAL REASONING

Materials: tens rods and unit cubes

- Read aloud the following riddle: **I am thinking of a number. The number has 2 tens. The ones digit is an even number between 7 and 9.**

- **What do you need to find out?** *the number you are thinking of* Reread the riddle; have students show what they know with rods and unit cubes. Then, have students solve the riddle.
- Read the riddle again. Does your answer make sense?

3•8 COMPARE NUMBERS

- Materials: sentence strips for is greater than, is less than, is equal to; 2-digit number cards
- Have 2 volunteers each pick a number card and face the group. Invite a third student to stand between them.
- Ask the group to help you compare the numbers. Give the *is greater than* strip to the volunteer in the middle. Have students read from left to right; for example, *21 is greater than 39.* Ask whether the statement is correct. Repeat until students determine which sign correctly compares the 2 numbers. Repeat with other numbers and volunteers.
- Use the symbols as well. Write >, <, and = on the reverse side of the signs and repeat the activity.

3•9 ORDER NUMBERS

Materials: number cards

- Have a volunteer stand and face the group. Give the student a number card, such as 48, to hold. Display 6 other cards on the chalkboard ledge, including those for 47 and 49.
- **What number comes before 48?** Have a volunteer take the correct number card and stand before the first student. **What number comes after 48?** Have a student stand on the other side. Repeat with other numbers.

3•10 SKIP COUNT

Materials: number line for 0–50, crayons, Activity Page 3-B

- Write 2 + 2 = _____ on the chalkboard. Have students call out the sum as you write and circle 4.

  Write 4 + 2 = _____ and repeat. Continue adding 2 to each new sum up to 10. Have students say 2, 4, 6, 8, 10 as you point to each number.
- Display a number line and mark 2, 4, 6, 8, 10. **What pattern do you see?** *skip over a number to get to the next number in the pattern* Have volunteers continue the pattern. Then have students count by twos from 2–50. Repeat the procedure to count by threes, fours, and fives.
- Distribute the activity page. Have students show the pattern for counting by twos, threes, fours, or fives by coloring squares. You may want to give each student 4 copies of the activity page so that they can show all 4 patterns.

3•11 Odd and Even Numbers

Materials: number cards 9–24, connecting cubes, counters, Activity Page 3-B

- Distribute number cards and a corresponding number of cubes to pairs of students. Have partners place their cubes in pairs. **Do you have any cubes left over?** Explain that if the answer is yes, the number on their card is odd; if the answer is no, the number is even. Have partners say their numbers as you record them on the chalkboard in 2 lists: odd and even. **How do the numbers in each list end?**
- Distribute activity pages and counters to partners. Have them use counters to cover all the even numbers so that only odd numbers show. Afterwards, repeat with even numbers.

3•12 Ordinal Numbers

Materials: word cards for first through twelfth, number cards 1st through 12th

- Hold up the word cards one at a time and read them with students. Explain that the words tell about position. To illustrate, have 12 volunteers form a line and face the door. Have students in turn take a card, read it, and give it to the volunteer who is in that position. Continue for all the cards. Then have students reread them in line order.
- Randomly distribute the number cards to 12 new volunteers. Have them arrange themselves in order, holding up their cards as they say their positions in line.

Activity Page 3-B

Name _____ Date _____

Counting Patterns/Odd and Even Numbers

1	2	3	4	5	6	7	8	9	10
11	12	13	14	15	16	17	18	19	20
21	22	23	24	25	26	27	28	29	30
31	32	33	34	35	36	37	38	39	40
41	42	43	44	45	46	47	48	49	50
51	52	53	54	55	56	57	58	59	60
61	62	63	64	65	66	67	68	69	70
71	72	73	74	75	76	77	78	79	80
81	82	83	84	85	86	87	88	89	90
91	92	93	94	95	96	97	98	99	100

CHAPTER 4 Money

CLUSTER A, PAGES 119-134

Objectives

- use coins to make money amounts up to 25¢
- order groups of coins to count
- count groups of coins that include half dollars
- show money amounts using the fewest coins
- count up from a price to make change
- recognize cause and effect

Cluster A Materials

- envelopes
- play coins
- price tags
- Activity Page 4-A

Math Words

Words	Examples
cent	¢
dime	10¢ ten cents
half dollar	50¢ fifty cents
nickel	5¢ five cents
penny	1¢ one cent

quarter

25¢
twenty-five cents

Teaching Strategies See pp. v–vi for teaching tips on working with ELL students.

4•1 COINS

Materials: per student: 2 dimes, 3 nickels, 5 pennies, 1 quarter; price tags with amounts up to 25¢

- Distribute coins. Review the value of each coin by having students hold up the coin that is worth 1¢, 5¢, 10¢, and 25¢.
- Display price tags. Call out a combination of coins to match an amount (go from greatest value to the least), and have students arrange their coins in a row. Count the coins together to find the total amount. Then, have students point to the corresponding price tag and say the amount. Repeat for the remaining amounts.

4•2 COUNTING MONEY

Materials: quarter, dime, nickel, penny; envelopes with groups of coins up to 50¢

- Hold up each coin for students to name and tell its value. Then have students name the coins in order from the greatest in value to the least. Write the names of the coins across the chalkboard as a reminder.
- Distribute envelopes to pairs of students who will remove the coins and arrange them in order starting with the greatest value. As you check the order, ask students to count the coins aloud and say the total.

4•3 HALF DOLLAR

Materials: envelopes with various combinations of pennies; nickels, dimes, and quarters, each totaling 50 cents

- Give an envelope to each pair of students. Have them order the coins from greatest to least value and then find the total. At your signal, have students call out the total. *50¢*
- Hold up a half dollar. Ask students to name the coin. Explain that a half dollar is worth half of a dollar, or 50¢. Give each pair of students a half dollar. Write amounts over 50 cents on the chalkboard. Have students use the half dollar and other coins to model the amounts.

4•4 COINS USED TO BUY

Materials: a variety of coins; 5 price tags marked 46¢, 58¢, 63¢, 78¢, 82¢, 99¢; Activity Page 4-A

- Attach price tags to classroom items. Distribute activity page 4-A and coins. Display the item tagged 46¢. Ask students to show (on the work mat on the activity page) the fewest number of coins to pay for it. *1 quarter, 2 dimes, 1 penny* Remind students to start with coins of the greatest value.
- Call on students to share their results. When they have determined the fewest number of coins to pay for the item, have students record the amount and the total number of coins they used. Repeat with the remaining items.

4•5 MAKE CHANGE

Materials: per student pair: an envelope with 1 quarter, 1 half dollar, 2 dimes, 1 nickel, and 4 pennies; 4 price tags marked 26¢, 58¢, 36¢, 41¢

- Attach price tags to classroom items. Distribute envelopes to partners. Have them role-play a store clerk with the pennies and a customer with the remaining coins.

- Display the item tagged 26¢. Have customers use the fewest coins to pay for it. **How much did you give the clerk?** *30¢* **What coins did you use?** *1 quarter, 1 nickel* **Do you get change back?** *yes*
- Have store clerks use pennies and count up to 30¢, starting with 26 and saying 27¢, 28¢, 29¢, 30¢. How much change did you give the customer? *4¢* Have partners trade roles and coins and repeat the procedure with other items.

4•6 READING FOR MATH: CAUSE AND EFFECT

- Write *cause* and *effect* on the chalkboard. Explain that *cause* is what makes something happen, and *effect* is what happens as a result.
- Write this story on the chalkboard: **Ann needed 75 cents more to buy a book. She walked the dog, set the table, and took out the trash for her brother to earn the money. He gave her 1 quarter, 4 dimes, 1 nickel, and 5 pennies. Ann bought the book after school.**
- **Why did Ann do her brother's chores? What happened as a result?**

Name _____   Date _____

Using the Fewest Coins to Pay

Use the work mat to figure out the fewest number of coins to pay for the item.

Write each amount. Write how many coins.

1. _____ ¢   2. _____ ¢   3. _____ ¢

_____ coins in all   _____ coins in all   _____ coins in all

4. _____ ¢   5. _____ ¢   6. _____ ¢

_____ coins in all   _____ coins in all   _____ coins in all

CLUSTER B, PAGES 135-145

Objectives

- use the strategy Act It Out to solve problems
- count dollars and cents
- compare amounts of money

Cluster B Materials

- bills and coins (play)
- envelopes
- price tags
- scissors
- tape or glue
- Activity Page 4-B

Math Words

Words	Examples
decimal point	.
dollar	$1 one dollar
dollar sign	$

Teaching Strategies See pp. v–vi for teaching tips on working with ELL students.

4•7 PROBLEM SOLVING STRATEGY: ACT IT OUT

Materials: scissors, glue, Activity Page 4-B
- Review the Four-Step Process: Read, Plan, Solve, Look Back.
- Write this problem on the chalkboard: **Max has 6 dimes and 12 nickels. In how many ways can he pay for a pencil that costs 30 cents?** Read the problem aloud. Have students suggest possible strategies they can use to solve it.

- If students do not suggest using coins to act out the problem, suggest it now. Then, distribute Activity Page 4-B and scissors. Have students cut out the coins at the bottom of the page and use them to model all the possible combinations of 30¢ to pay for the pencil. Students can then paste the coins on the chart. *3 dimes; 2 dimes and 2 nickels; 1 dime and 4 nickels; 6 nickels*

4•8 DOLLARS AND CENTS

Materials: per student: one envelope with 4 dollar bills, 1 half dollar, 3 quarters, 2 dimes, 4 nickels, 5 pennies; price tags with amounts between $1.25 and $4.75
- Distribute bills and coins. Review the value of each by having students hold up the bill or coins that are worth $1.00, 50¢, 25¢, 10¢, 5¢, and 1¢. Then write $1.05 on the chalkboard. Have students name each symbol as you point to it.
- Display price tags. Call out a combination of coins to match an amount and have students arrange their bills and coins in a row. Count the coins together to find the total amount. Then, have students point to the corresponding price tag and say the amount. Repeat for the remaining amounts.

4•9 COMPARE MONEY

Materials: per student: an envelope with a variety of bills and coins to illustrate amounts between $1.05 and $3.25; 8 price tags marked $1.10, $1.35, $1.95, $2.25, $2.60, $2.85, $3.05, $3.20
- Distribute envelopes. Display a tagged classroom item such as a book for $1.35. Ask students to say the amount.
- Instruct students to count the money in their envelopes. Remind them to arrange the bills and coins in order from the greatest to the least in value. **Do you have enough to buy the item? How much money do you have?** Have students say if they have enough money and tell the amount.
- Have students put the money back in the envelope and trade envelopes. Repeat the activity with the remaining items.

Name _____ Date _____

Showing Different Ways to Count Out 30¢

Cut out the coins.

Show all the ways to count out 30¢ with the coins.

Then paste the coins on the chart.

1.
2.

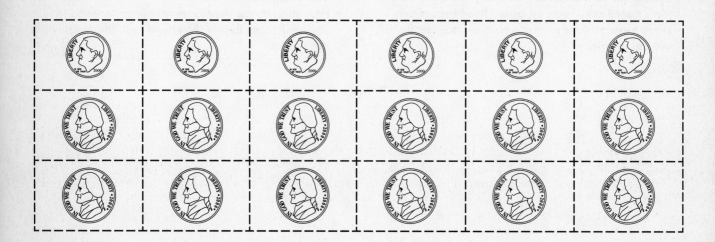

CHAPTER 5 Add 2 Digit Numbers

CLUSTER A, PAGES 155-174

Objectives

- add multiples of 10 to 2-digit numbers
- use basic facts to add tens and ones
- decide if regrouping is needed before adding 2 numbers
- add 2 numbers, regrouping when needed
- practice adding 2-digit numbers with and without regrouping
- identify important information to solve a problem

Cluster A Materials

- hundred chart
- index cards

- red, yellow, and blue connecting cubes
- tens rods and unit cubes
- Activity Page 5-A

Math Words

Words	Examples
addend	14 ← addend +12 ← addend 26
regroup	12 ones =1 ten 2 ones
sum	14 + 12 26 ← sum

Teaching Strategies See pp. v–vi for teaching tips on working with ELL students.

5•1 ADD TENS

Materials: ten rods and unit cubes, hundred chart

- Distribute ten rods and unit cubes to partners. Have one partner demonstrate 3 tens 2 ones. Have the other partner add on 3 tens, 1 at a time, saying 4 tens 2 ones, 5 tens 2 ones, 6 tens 2 ones. **How many tens and ones are there in all?** *6 tens 2 ones* **Write 32 + 30 = 62 on the chalkboard.**

- Display a hundred chart. Tell students they can also use a hundred chart to count on tens. Ask a volunteer to find 32 and count on 3 tens, saying 42, 52, 62. Have partners take turns counting on tens using a hundred chart to add 25 + 20, 37 + 50, 59 + 40, 13 + 10, 16 + 30, 36 + 60.

5•2 2-DIGIT ADDITION WITHOUT REGROUPING

Materials: ten rods and unit cubes

- Distribute rods and cubes to pairs of students. Write 32 + 16 vertically on the chalkboard. Draw a line between the tens and ones; have a volunteer label the columns *Tens and Ones.*

- Have each partner model an addend. **To solve the problem, what should you add first?** *ones* Have one partner put the ones together and tell how many. *8* Then have the other partner put the tens together and tell how many. *4* Ask a volunteer to say the sum and write the answer on the chalkboard to complete the problem. *48* Repeat the activity with other 2-digit addition problems that do not require regrouping.

5•3 DECIDE WHEN TO REGROUP

Materials: connecting cubes

- Give each pair of students 30 connecting cubes. Have one partner model 1 ten 8 ones. Have the other partner add 5 more ones and then tell how many tens and ones *1 ten 13 ones* **Do you need to regroup?** *yes* **Why?** *There are more than 10 ones.* Have partners make a ten. **How many ones are left?** *3* **How many tens and ones do you have in all?** *2 tens 3 ones* Write 18 + 5 = 23 on the chalkboard, pointing out that they just modeled this problem.

- Repeat the procedure with a problem that does not require regrouping, such as 22 + 7.

5•4 2-DIGIT ADDITION

Materials: ten rods and unit cubes

Draw a place value chart on the chalkboard. Have students pick two addends between 11 and 49, such as 25 and 48. Write them in the chart and have students model the addends with ten rods and unit cubes.

- Have students combine the ones. **Are there enough ones to regroup?** *yes* **How do you regroup 13 ones?** *Trade 10 ones for 1 ten and put it in the tens box.* **How many ones are left?** *3* Write *3* in the ones place. **How**

can you remember that you regrouped 10 ones for
1 ten when you add? *Write 1 in the tens box.* Write 1
on the chalkboard. Then have students combine their
tens. **How many tens do you have?** 7 Show how to
add the tens on the chalkboard and write 7. **What is
the sum?** *73*

5•5 MORE 2-DIGIT ADDITION

Materials: per pair of students: 10 index cards cut in half,
Activity Page 5-A, ten rods and unit cubes
- Have partners write the following numbers on cards:
  4–9, 11–19, 26, 33, 37, 44, 49 then, place them facedown in 2 piles of ten.
- Invite partners to each pick a card, model the number,
  and write the 2 numbers as addends on their Activity
  Pages. Before partners add, ask **Will you add tens first
  or ones?** *ones* **When will you regroup?** *when there are
  10 or more ones* **How will you show that you
  regrouped 10 ones as 1 ten?** *Write a 1 in the tens column.* Have partners complete the problem, using rods
  and cubes to model.

5•6 PRACTICE 2-DIGIT ADDITION

Materials: ten rods and unit cubes, Activity Page 5-A
- Have students work in pairs. Have one partner begin by
  using the rods and cubes to show 2 numbers between

11 and 49. Ask the other partner to look at each group
of rods and cubes and write on Activity Page 5-A the
numbers they represent as addends. At your signal, have
the partner with rods and cubes use them to add while
the other partner works on paper.
- Have partners compare their answers, each telling the
  other how he or she added to find the sum.

5•7 READING FOR MATH: IMPORTANT AND UNIMPORTANT INFORMATION

Materials: red, yellow, and blue connecting cubes
- Write on the chalkboard: **I have some cubes. They
  are different colors. I have 9 red cubes. I have the
  same number of yellow cubes. I like the blue cubes.
  I have 4 fewer blue cubes than red cubes or yellow
  cubes. How many cubes do I have in all?**
- Read the problem aloud. Have students identify those
  sentences that contain information they need to solve
  the problem. *sentences 3, 4, 6, 7*
- Have students use cubes and the information in the
  remaining sentences to solve the problem. *25 cubes in all*

Activity Page 5-A

Name _____ Date _____

Adding Tens and Ones

Use the Tens and Ones boxes to write and solve addition problems.

Tens	Ones
□	
+	

Tens	Ones
□	
+	

Tens	Ones
□	
+	

4.

Tens	Ones
□	
+	

5.

Tens	Ones
□	
+	

6.

Tens	Ones
□	
+	

7.

Tens	Ones
□	
+	

8.

Tens	Ones
□	
+	

9.

Tens	Ones
□	
+	

CLUSTER B, PAGES 175-189

Objectives

- draw a picture to solve problems
- check addition by reversing the order of addends
- estimate sums by finding the nearest ten
- add money amounts to 99¢
- add three 2-digit numbers

Cluster B Materials

- crayons
- index cards
- number line
- play coins
- price tags
- small self-stick notes
- Activity Page 5-B

Math Words

Words	Examples
Estimate	28 + 42
	30 + 40
	30 + 40
	about 70 ← estimate

Teaching Strategies See pp. v–vi for teaching tips on working with ELL students.

5•8 PROBLEM SOLVING STRATEGY: DRAW A PICTURE

Materials: crayons, Activity Page 5-B

- Write this problem on the chalkboard and read it aloud: **The children are picking flowers for their mother. Lisa picks 16 yellow flowers. Mark picks 18 red flowers. How many flowers do the children pick in all?** Ask students to suggest possible problem-solving strategies, such as acting it out or drawing a picture.
- Distribute Activity Page 5-B. Reread the problem. **What facts do you know?** *The children picked 16 yellow flowers and 18 red flowers.* **What are you asked to find?** *how many flowers in all* Have students use the activity page to record.
- Remind students that drawing a picture is one strategy they can use to solve a problem. Have them draw a picture on their activity page and solve. Have volunteers display their drawings and tell how they helped students solve the problem.

5•9 ALGEBRA: CHECK ADDITION

Materials: index cards

- Write these problems in vertical form on 2 index cards: 25 + 14 and 14 + 25. Have 2 volunteers come to the chalkboard. Give each a card and a piece of chalk. At your signal, tell them to write the problem and find the sum. Remind students to add ones first.
- Focus attention on the completed problems. **How are the problems the same?** *Addends and sums are the same.* **Different?** *The order of the addends is different.* Then ask students how they might use this information. *They can use the information to check addition answers.*
- Repeat with new pairs of problems and students.

5•10 ESTIMATE SUMS

Materials: number line, small self-stick notes

- Write 28 + 13 in vertical form on the chalkboard. Have students copy and add.
- Display a number line on the chalkboard to show tens from 0–50. Write 28 and 13 on self-stick notes. Have 2 volunteers stand near the number line. Give each a number. **Is 28 nearer to 20 or 30? Is 13 nearer to 10 or 20?** Have volunteers place the numbers on the line about where they belong.
- Next, write 30 + 10 in vertical form. Explain that you rewrote 28 and 13 to the nearest ten. Have students copy and add and then compare the 2 sums. **Are your 2 sums close?** Explain that if the answer is yes, then the sum of 28 + 13 is reasonable. Repeat with other addends.

5•11 ADD MONEY AMOUNTS

Materials: dimes and pennies, price tags

- Tag several items and distribute coins. Display 2 tagged items, such as a box of crayons for 28¢ and a book for 45¢. Point to each tag, and have students say the amount.
- Have students model how many dimes and pennies they need to buy each item. *2 dimes, 8 pennies; 4 dimes, 5 pennies* Next, have students combine the pennies, regrouping 10 pennies as 1 dime. Then have students combine the dimes. **How many dimes and pennies are there in all?** *7 dimes, 3 pennies*
- Write 28¢ + 45¢ in vertical form on the chalkboard, and find the sum together. Encourage students to tell how adding dimes and pennies is like adding tens and ones.

5•12 THREE ADDENDS

Materials: Activity Page 5-B

- Write 32 + 16 + 24 in vertical form on the chalkboard. As you point to each addend, have students say the number. Then ask students to copy the problem on paper. Point out that looking for doubles or a way to make a 10 can make adding 3 numbers easier.
- Ask students to look at the ones and raise their hands when they see a way to make a 10. Have a volunteer

circle the 2 numbers and say them aloud. Write 10 next to the 6 and 4. **Where can you show this ten? How?** *Write a 1 in the tens column.* Show this and have students do the same. **How many ones are left?** *2* Write 2. Have students do the same. Then have them add the tens. **What is the sum?** *72*

• Write 23 + 15 + 43 in vertical form on the chalkboard. This time, have students identify and circle the doubles, add 6 ones + 5 ones, regrouping 11 ones as 1 ten 1 one, write a 1 in the tens column, and then add.

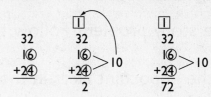

Activity Page 5-B

Drawing a Picture to Solve a Problem

Read the story problem. Follow the directions.

1. Find the important facts in the story. List them.

_____

_____

2. Find the question. Write what it asks you to find.

_____

3. Draw a picture to help solve the problem.

_____

4. Write a sentence to answer the question in the problem.

_____

CHAPTER 6 Subtract 2-Digit Numbers

CLUSTER A, PAGES 199-218

Objectives

- subtract multiples of 10 from 2-digit numbers
- use basic facts to subtract tens and ones
- decide if regrouping is needed before subtracting 2 numbers
- subtract, regrouping 1 ten as 10 ones as needed
- practice 2-digit subtraction with and without regrouping
- name the steps in a process

Cluster A Materials

- base-ten cubes
- base-ten rods
- connecting cubes
- construction paper in 2 colors
- hundred chart
- sentence strips
- Activity Page 6-A

Math Words

Words	Examples
difference	47 − 28 19 ← difference
regroup	1 ten 4 ones = 14 ones

Teaching Strategies See pp. v–vi for teaching tips on working with ELL students.

6•1 SUBTRACT TENS

Materials: tens rods and unit cubes (or plastic straws and elastic bands), hundred chart

- Display a hundred chart, and distribute tens rods and unit cubes to partners. Have one partner show 5 tens 4 ones. Have the other partner then subtract 3 tens,

counting back aloud, saying how many tens and ones are left each time. *4 tens 4 ones, 3 tens 4 ones, 2 tens 4 ones* Write 54 − 30 = 24 vertically on the chalkboard, pointing out that students just demonstrated this problem.

- Tell students that they can also use a hundred chart to count back tens. Ask a volunteer to find 54 and count back 3 tens, saying 44, 34, 24. Have partners take turns counting back tens using a hundred chart to subtract 55 − 20, 97 − 50, 49 − 40, 36 − 10, 81 − 30, 88 − 20 and showing the problems with tens rods and unit cubes.

6•2 2-DIGIT SUBTRACTION WITHOUT REGROUPING

Materials: tens rods and unit cubes (or connecting cubes or plastic straws and elastic bands)

- Write 67 − 23 vertically on the chalkboard, draw a line between the tens and ones, and ask a volunteer to label the columns *tens* and *ones*.
- Have students work in pairs. Ask one partner to use tens rods and unit cubes to show 67. **To solve the problem, which do you do first, subtract tens or ones?** *ones* Have the other partner take away 3 ones. **How many units are left?** *4* Then, have the first partner take away 2 tens and tell how many are left. *4* Have a volunteer say the difference as you write it on the chalkboard.
- Repeat with other 2-digit subtraction problems not requiring regrouping.

6•3 DECIDE WHEN TO REGROUP

Materials: connecting cubes

- Give each pair of students 40 connecting cubes. After one partner shows 3 tens 6 ones, the other partner will subtract 9 ones. **Do you need to regroup?** *yes* **Why?** *There are not enough ones.* Have the first partner take apart 1 ten to make 10 ones and add them to the 6 ones. **Are there enough ones to subtract now?** *yes* **How many ones are there?** *16* Have the other partner subtract 9 ones. **How many ones are left?** *7* **How many tens and ones do you have now?** *2 tens 7 ones* Write 36 − 9 = 27 on the chalkboard, pointing out that students just demonstrated this problem.
- Repeat the procedure with a problem that does not require regrouping, such as 28 − 7. Have partners reverse roles.

6•4 2-DIGIT SUBTRACTION

Materials: tens rods and unit cubes

- Draw a place value chart on the chalkboard. Write a 2-digit number between 51 and 55, such as 53, on the chart. Ask students to use their tens rods and unit cubes to show this number. Then, write -16 on the chart to complete the subtraction problem.

- Point to the 6, and tell students you want them to subtract 6 ones from their model. **Do you have enough units?** *no* **What must you do?** *Regroup 1 ten as 10 ones.* Have students remove 1 ten, take 10 ones to replace it, and combine them with the 3 ones. **How can you show this in the problem on the chalkboard?** *Cross out the 5 and 3, write 4 in the tens column, and write 16 in the ones column.* Show this on the chalkboard.
- Have students subtract 9 ones from the 16 ones and 1 ten from the 4 tens. **How many tens and ones are left?** *3 tens 7 ones* **How can you show this difference in the problem?** *write 37* Have a volunteer write the difference.

6•5 MORE 2-DIGIT SUBTRACTION

Materials: 4″ construction-paper squares in 2 colors, tens rods and unit cubes, Activity Page 6-A

- Working in pairs, have one partner write 52, 53, 54, 65, 66, 77, 78, 81, and 89 on squares of one color while the other partner writes 11, 12, 13, 14, 25, 26, 27, 38, and 39 on the remaining squares. Have partners combine their squares, mix them up, and place them facedown in a pile.
- Let each partner pick a card, use ones and tens models to show the number, and then write the numbers on their Activity Pages to make a subtraction problem. **Which number will you write first?** *the greater number* Before partners subtract, ask: **Will you subtract tens first or ones?** *ones* **When will you regroup?** *when there are not enough ones to subtract* **What will you do to show you have regrouped?** *Cross out the top tens and ones digits and write the new numbers in the*

boxes. Have partners complete the problem, using the tens rods and unit cubes to show their work.

6•6 PRACTICE 2-DIGIT SUBTRACTION

Materials: tens rods and unit cubes

- Have students work in pairs. Let one partner choose 2 numbers to make a subtraction problem, one between 61 and 91 and the other between 19 and 49. Have partners write the problem on their paper and use tens rods and unit cubes to show the greater number. At your signal, have one partner use tens rods and unit cubes to subtract as the other partner subtracts on paper. Have partners compare their answers, each telling the other how he or she subtracted to find the difference.
- Have partners switch roles and repeat with 2 new numbers between 61 and 91 and 19 and 49.

6•7 READING FOR MATH: STEPS IN A PROCESS

Materials: sentence strips

- Write the following story on 5 sentence strips: **Max and Ann arranged the bookshelves. First, they sorted the books and magazines. Next, they put 35 picture books on the bottom shelf. After that, they put 47 information books on the middle shelf. Finally, they put 28 magazines on the top shelf.** Randomly arrange the sentences on a bulletin chalkboard.
- Lead students in reading the sentences aloud. Have them help you put the sentences in the correct order using the words *First, Next, After that,* and *Finally* as clues.
- Ask students to make up subtraction problems about the story and then take turns reading and solving the problems.

Activity Page 6-A

Name _____ Date _____

Subtracting Tens and Ones

Use the tens and ones boxes to write and solve subtraction problems.

Tens	Ones
□	
−	

Tens	Ones
□	
−	

Tens	Ones
□	
−	

4.

Tens	Ones
□	
−	

5.

Tens	Ones
□	
−	

6.

Tens	Ones
□	
−	

7.

Tens	Ones
□	
−	

8.

Tens	Ones
□	
−	

9.

Tens	Ones
□	
−	

CLUSTER B, PAGES 219–232

Objectives

- **choose the operation to solve a problem**
- **check subtraction by adding**
- **estimate to see if differences are reasonable**
- **subtract amounts of money**

Cluster B Materials

- index cards
- number line
- play dimes and pennies
- tagchalkboard price tag
- Activity Page 6-B

Math Word

Words	Examples
estimate	42 – 28
	40 – 30
	about 10 estimate

Teaching Strategies See pp. v–vi for teaching tips on working with ELL students.

6•8 PROBLEM SOLVING STRATEGY: CHOOSE THE OPERATION

- Review the Four-Step Process: Read, Plan, Solve, Look Back.
- Write this problem on the chalkboard and read it aloud: **A group of children picked apples. Ed picked 18 red apples. Meg picked 25 green apples. How many more green apples than red apples did they pick?**
- **What facts do you know?** *how many apples each child picked* Have a volunteer circle *18 red apples* and *25 green apples*. **What do you need to find out?** *how many more green apples than red apples* Have a volunteer underline the question. Have students suggest possible problem-solving strategies to use, such as acting it out or drawing a picture. **What else must you decide to solve the problem?** *whether to add or subtract* Read the question aloud. Have students say the words that let them know which operation to use. *how many more. . . than*
- Have students solve the problem on paper, using any strategy they choose. **How many apples did the children pick in all?** Have them choose the correct operation and solve.

6•9 CHECK SUBTRACTION

Materials: index cards

- Write 25 – 7 and 18 + 7 vertically, each on a separate index card. Give the cards to 2 volunteers and have them follow the signs and add or subtract. Remind them to add or subtract ones first, regroup if necessary, and then add or subtract tens. When both students are finished, have them come to the chalkboard and copy their problems and answers.
- Have all students look at the completed problems and tell what they notice. *The difference and one addend are the same; all the numbers are the same, but in a different order.*
- Repeat with another pair of students and the problems 38 – 13 and 25 + 13. Then, ask students how they might use what they have learned to check their subtraction.

6•10 ESTIMATE DIFFERENCES

Materials: number line

- Write 48 – 19 vertically on the chalkboard. Have students copy the problem and subtract. Have a volunteer work at the chalkboard.
- Display a number line on the chalkboard that shows tens from 0 – 50. **Which ten is nearer to 48, 40 or 50?** *50* **Which ten is nearer to 19, 10 or 20?** *20*
- Write 50 – 20 vertically on the chalkboard. Explain that you rewrote 48 and 19 to the nearest ten. Have students copy and subtract and then compare the two differences as the volunteer works at the chalkboard. **Are the two differences close?** Explain that if the answer is yes, then the answer is reasonable. Repeat with other subtraction problems.

6•11 SUBTRACT MONEY AMOUNTS

Materials: price tag, play dimes and pennies, Activity Page 6-B

- Tell students to pretend that they have 50¢. Display a pen with a price tag marked 29¢, and have students tell the price in a sentence. Have students pretend that they just bought the pen. **How can you find out how much change you get back?** *subtract*
- Write 50¢ – 29¢ vertically on the chalkboard. Have students use dimes and pennies to show the subtraction. Ask what they must do before they can subtract ones. *Regroup 1 dime as 10 pennies to make 4 dimes and 10 pennies.* Have a volunteer complete the problem on the chalkboard, crossing out 5 and 0, writing 4 and 10 to show the regrouping and the answer. *21¢*
- Distribute Activity Page 6-B. Have students pretend that they have been shopping, the coins show how much they paid, and the price tag tells what each item costs. Have them write a subtraction problem to find how much change they get back. They can use dimes and pennies to show each problem.
- Discuss the problem as a group. Extend the activity by inviting students to suggest additional problems.

Activity Page 6-B

Name _____ Date _____

Subtracting Money Amounts

Write how much you pay. Write how much each item costs.

Subtract to find out how much change you get back.

28¢

_____ ¢

− _____ ¢

_____ ¢

59¢

_____ ¢

− _____ ¢

_____ ¢

33¢

_____ ¢

− _____ ¢

_____ ¢

JUICE 76¢

_____ ¢

− _____ ¢

_____ ¢

CLUSTER A, PAGES 241-254

Objectives

- tell time to the hour and half hour
- tell time to five-minute intervals
- tell time to the quarter hour
- tell time in different ways
- use sequence of events to answer questions about a story

Cluster A Materials

- demonstration analog clock   • Activity Page 7-A

Math Words

Words	Examples
half hour	
hour	
minute	
quarter hour	

Teaching Strategies See pp. v–vi for teaching tips on working with ELL students.

7•1 TIME TO THE HOUR AND HALF HOUR

Materials: demonstration analog clock
- Set the clock to 9 o'clock. Ask students to identify each hand as you point to it and then tell what time it is.

Next, have students count by ones as you move the minute hand around the clock once and the hour hand to 10. **How long does it take for the minute hand to move around the clock once and the hour hand to move from 9 to 10?** *60 minutes; one hour* **What time does the clock show now?** *10 o'clock* Draw 2 digital clocks on the chalkboard; write 9:00 on one clock and 10:00 on the other.

- Follow a similar procedure to demonstrate time to the half hour, starting at 10 o'clock. Students should note that the minute hand is on 6 and the hour hand is halfway between 10 and 11 at 10:30.
- Using one of the digital clocks on the chalkboard, write times to the hour and half hour for students to read. Then, call on volunteers to move the hands on the demonstration analog clock to model each time.

7•2 TIME TO 5 MINUTES

Materials: demonstration analog clock
- Display a demonstration clock set to 12 o'clock. Have students count by fives as you move the minute hand from 1 to 12 and the hour hand to 1. Reinforce the fact that as the minute hand moves between 12 and 1, 1 and 2, 2 and 3, and so on, 5 minutes pass by.
- Ask a volunteer to show 8 o'clock on the clock. Have students count by fives to 35 as you move the minute hand at 5-minute intervals to 7 and then say the time. *8:35*
- Draw a digital clock on the chalkboard. Call on pairs of students. Have one student show a time to 5 minutes on the demonstration clock, such as 9:55. Have the other student say and write the time on the digital clock. Have students trade clocks and repeat.

7•3 TIME TO THE QUARTER HOUR

Materials: demonstration analog clock
- Gather students around the demonstration clock. Ask where the minute and hour hands should be if it were 9 o'clock. *on 12; on 9* Have a volunteer move the clock hands to show 9 o'clock. Then, have the volunteer move the minute hand ahead by 15 minutes or a quarter hour, counting by fives. **Where should the minute hand be?** *on 3* **What time is it?** *3:15* **What time should it be if we move the minute hand ahead another quarter hour?** *3:30* Repeat 2 more times to 10 o'clock. You may wish to draw a digital clock on the chalkboard to record each time.
- Call on 5 students at a time to form a circle. Have 1 student begin by showing a time on the hour, such as 3

o'clock. Have each student in turn show the next quarter hour and say the time.

7•4 MORE TIME

Materials: demonstration analog clock, Activity Page 7-A
- Instruct a volunteer as follows: Position the hour hand between 8 and 9 and the minute hand at 7. **What time is it?** *8:35* Write 8:35 on the chalkboard. **How many minutes after eight is it?** Write 35 minutes after 8. **How many minutes before 9 is it?** Write 25 minutes before 9. Emphasize that students can use all 3 ways to tell the time.
- Repeat the procedure to model 11:15/quarter after. Remind students to count by fives, if necessary.
- Distribute Activity Page 7-A. For items 1 and 2, have students draw the hands on the clock and write each time 3 ways. For item 3, have students make up their own time and cut along the dotted lines. Students can then trade papers and complete the activity.

7•5 READING FOR MATH: SEQUENCE OF EVENTS

- Write the following on the chalkboard: Max gets up at quarter after 6 on school days. He gets dressed first. Then he eats breakfast at 30 minutes after 6. He leaves the house at 5 minutes before 7 to meet his friends. Their bus comes at 10 minutes after 7.
- Read the story aloud with students. Call on volunteers to underline each mention of time in the story. Have students use their clocks to show each time and say it a different way. Then list these times on the chalkboard: 6:15, 6:30, 6:55, and 7:10. **When does the day begin for Max? What does Max do at 6:30? At what time does Max leave the house? When does his bus come?** Write what Max does next to the correct time. **Is it more than an hour or less than an hour between the time Max gets up and the school bus comes?** Encourage students to use the clocks and the information on the chalkboard to figure out the answer.

Activity Page 7-A

Name _____   Date _____

Telling Time

Draw the hands on the clock.

Use blue for the minute hand.

Use red for the hour hand.

Then write each time 3 different ways.

1. The minute hand points to 8.
   The hour hand is between 5 and 6.

   _____ minutes after _____

   _____ minutes before _____

_____

2. The minute hand points to 3.
   The hour hand points to 11.

   _____ : _____

   quarter after _____

   _____ minutes before _____

   _____ minutes after _____

3. Now make up your own, then cut along the line.
   Trade with a partner. Write the time at least 2 ways.

- -

   The minute hand points to _____ .

   The hour hand points to _____ .

CLUSTER B, PAGES 255-266

Objectives

- solve problems about time relationships
- solve problems about elapsed time
- use a calendar

Cluster B Materials

- crayons
- demonstration analog clock
- index cards
- old wall calendars
- paper fasteners (brads)
- paper plates
- tagchalkboard
- Activity Page 7-B

Math Words

Words	Examples
calendar	**JANUARY 2001** Sun Mon Tues Wed Thu Fri Sat 1 2 3 4 5 6 7 8 9 10 11 12 13 14 15 16 17 18 19 20 21 22 23 24 25 26 27 28 29 30 31
month	January
week	Sun Mon Tues Wed Thu Fri Sat 1 2 3 4 5 6 7
year	2001

Teaching Strategies See pp. v–vi for teaching tips on working with ELL students.

7•6 PROBLEM SOLVING STRATEGY: ACT IT OUT

Materials: demonstration analog clock

- Write this problem on the chalkboard and read it aloud: Ann had to do her math homework, walk the dog, and clean her room. Each job took 20 minutes. How long did the 3 jobs take?
- **What do you know?** *Ann has 3 jobs to do; each job takes 20 minutes.* Have a volunteer circle the facts in the story. **What do you need to find out?** *how long the 3 jobs take* Have a volunteer underline the question.
- Have students use a clock to act out the story and solve the problem. The 3 jobs took 60 minutes or 1 hour.

7•7 ELAPSED TIME

Materials: demonstration analog clock, paper plates, tagchalkboard minute and hour hands, paper fasteners, index cards, Activity Page 7-B

- Make or have students make a paper plate clock face. After writing the numbers, have students use a fastener to attach the minute and hour hands.
- Show 6 o'clock on the demonstration clock. Ask students to watch as you move the minute hand around the clock one time and the hour hand from 6 to 7, explaining that it is now 1 hour later. **What time is it 1 hour later?** *7 o'clock* Repeat to show 2 hours and 3 hours later.
- Have students work in pairs. Give partners 2 activity pages and an index card with a start time and an end time of 1 hour, 2 hours, or 3 hours later. For example, start time: 9 o'clock; end time: 12 o'clock. Have one partner show the start time and the other the end time. Then, have partners decide if the end time is 1 hour, 2 hours, or 3 hours later. Have partners hold up their clocks, say the start and end times, and give the elapsed time. Partners can trade cards to continue. Repeat 3 times.
- Have students use their activity pages to record the start and end times, draw hands on the each clock to show the start and end time, and then circle the correct elapsed time.

7•8 CALENDAR

Materials: old wall calendars for each month of the year, crayons

- Give each student a calendar. Begin by having 12 volunteers each with a different month come to the front of the room. At your signal, ask them to arrange themselves in order from January to December.
- Have seated students answer questions such as: What is the month just after July? What is the month just before April? What is the fifth month? Which months are between May and August? What is the eleventh month? Which month has fewer than 30 days? Which months have 30 days?
- After volunteers are seated, have all students do the following on their calendars: Underline the name of the month. If the calendar has the year, circle it with a red crayon. Make a blue X on the last day of the month. Use a green crayon to color in the first day of the month and circle the day of the week on which it falls.

Activity Page 7-B

Name _____   Date _____

Showing Elapsed Time

Write the start time. Draw the hands on the clock.

Write the end time. Draw the hands on the clock.

How many hours later is it? Circle your choice.

   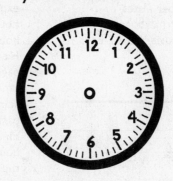   1 hour later

2 hours later

3 hours later

start time _____ : _____   end time _____ : _____

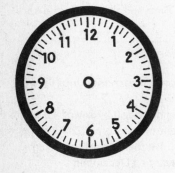      1 hour later

2 hours later

3 hours later

start time _____ : _____   end time _____ : _____

   1 hour later

2 hours later

3 hours later

start time _____ : _____   end time _____ : _____

CHAPTER 8 Data and Graphs

Objectives

- read and interpret pictographs
- take a survey and use tallies to record results
- practice reading, interpreting, and making bar graphs
- use diagrams to solve problems and draw conclusions

Cluster A Materials

- chalk
- chart paper
- crayons or markers
- pictures of broccoli, string beans, spinach, peas, or other green vegetables

- pictures of 4 seasons
- pictures of people in-line skating and ice skating
- Activity Page 8-A

Math Words

Words	Examples
bar graph	Show students a sample **bar graph.**
chart	Show students a sample tally **chart.**
data	collected information Show students the **data** collected for a class survey.
pictograph	Show students a sample **pictograph.**
tally mark	Show students a sample tally table with **tally marks** in place.

Teaching Strategies See pp. v–vi for teaching tips on working with ELL students.

8•1 READ PICTOGRAPHS

Materials: chalk, pictures of green vegetables
- Display and identify pictures of 4 green vegetables. Make a 4-row graph entitled "Our Favorite Green Vegetables." Write the name of a green vegetable to the left of each row. Have students name their favorite and draw smiling faces in the corresponding rows. Tell students they have just made a pictograph, a kind of graph that uses pictures to compare information, or data.

- Have students tell how many green vegetables the graph shows and what each smiling face stands for. *4; I student* Then, have students count the number of pictures for each vegetable and use the data to answer questions such as these: **How many students voted? Which vegetable do most students like best? How many students like peas and string beans? How many more students like peas than broccoli?**

8•2 TALLY MARKS AND CHARTS

Materials: chart paper, crayons or markers
- Tell students you are taking a survey. Ask which subject they like best—math, science, social studies, or reading. Begin a list of their choices on the chalkboard. After several responses, explain that there is an easier way to take a survey. Tell students you will make a chart.
- Write "Our Favorite Subjects" on chart paper. Ask how many rows are needed to show all the subjects students can choose from. *4* Make 4 rows, and write math, science, social studies, and reading. Demonstrate how to make tally marks. Then, have students make I tally mark each next to their favorite subject. Count the tally marks together and record the total at the end of each row. Then, ask questions similar to the following: Which subject does the class like best? **Which subject does the class like least? How many more students picked science than reading as their favorite?** (Save the chart for Cluster B Activity 8•6.)
- Have students create complete sentences based on the data in their graphs.

8•3 BAR GRAPHS

Materials: pictures of the seasons, Activity Page 8-A
- Display pictures, and have students name the seasons. Explain that you want to make a bar graph to show the results of a favorite-seasons survey. Write *bar graph* on the chalkboard. Then list the following: summer-9, fall-4, winter-7, spring-6.
- Distribute activity pages. Work together to complete the bar graph. Have students suggest a title such as "Favorite Seasons" and record the names of the seasons. Then, point out the data on the chalkboard and have students fill in the correct number of spaces for each season. Have students use the completed bar graph to answer these questions: **Does the graph show that students liked winter more than summer?** *no* **Is the total for summer and fall equal to the total for winter and spring?** *yes* **Which season did the fewest students vote for?** *fall*

- Have students create complete sentences based on the data in their graphs.

8•4 READING FOR MATH: DRAW CONCLUSIONS

Materials: chalk, pictures of people skating
- Display the pictures. Do you like to ice skate or to in-line skate? Draw two large overlapping circles to make a Venn diagram. Write "ice skate" under one circle, "in-line skate" under the other, and "both" where they overlap. Have students tell which activity they like, or whether they like both, and then write their name in the appropriate circle.
- Have students use the diagram to answer questions such as the following: **How many students like to ice skate (or in-line skate or do both)? How do you know?** *count the names* **Do more students like to in-line skate than to ice skate? How do you know?** *count and compare*
- Challenge students to show how they would represent someone who liked neither activity.

Activity Page 8-A

Name _____ Date _____

Making a Bar Graph

Finish the bar graph. Write a title and the name of each season. Fill in the correct number of spaces.

Use the data on the chalkboard.

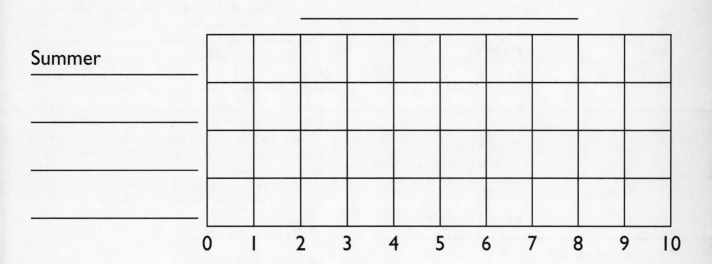

Summer

CLUSTER B, PAGES 287-297

Objectives

- use a table to solve problems
- use the same data in more than one way
- practice finding the range and mode of a set of data

Cluster B Materials

- chalk
- chart from Activity 8•2
- chart paper
- crayons or markers
- number cards
- play dollar bills (optional)
- Activity Page 8-B

Math Words

Words	Examples
mode	3 6 12 6 the number that occurs most often
range	3 6 12 6 12 – 3 = 9 the difference between the greatest and the least in a set of data
set	3 6 12 6 a set of data

Teaching Strategies See pp. v–vi for teaching tips on working with ELL students.

8•5 PROBLEM SOLVING STRATEGY: USE A TABLE

Materials: chalk, play dollar bills (optional)

- Read the following story problemaloud: **Sam wants a game that costs $25. He began saving the money he earns 4 weeks ago. He earned $6 the first week. He earned $4 the second week. He earned $8 last week. This week he earned $7. Does Sam have enough money to buy the game?**
- Explain that one way to solve the problem is to organize the data in a table. Begin a table on the chalkboard entitled "Sam's Game Money." Label the first row "Week" and the second row "How Much." Make 4 columns. Use the table on page 287 as a model. As you reread the problem, have volunteers fill in the data. 1, 2, 3, 4; $6, $4, $8, $7

- Ask students to recall how much the game costs and what they are to find out. *$25; if Sam has enough money to buy the game* Then, ask what data they will use and how they will use it to solve the problem. *add together the 4 amounts* Have students use paper and pencil to solve. Students can also use play money.

8•6 REPRESENT DATA IN DIFFERENT WAYS

Materials: chart from Activity 8•2, chart paper, markers or crayons, Activity Page 8-B

- Display "Our Favorite Subjects" chart from Activity 8•2. Explain that the same data can be shown on a pictograph. Start a pictograph on chart paper. Copy the title and 4 subjects. **What picture can you use instead of a tally mark to show each vote?** example: *smiling face* Have students tell how many of each picture they need to draw for each subject. Have volunteers finish the chart.
- Explain that the same data can also be shown in a bar graph. Distribute activity pages. Have students write the title and subjects. Ask how they will show each vote instead of a tally mark or picture. *fill in a space* Have students complete the bar graph using the same data as on the tally chart .
- Conclude by having students tell how the chart, pictograph, and bar graph are alike and different.

8•7 RANGE AND MODE

Materials: number cards

- Distribute the following number cards to volunteers: 3, 9, 10, 9, 28. Have the volunteers stand in front of the class. Ask the rest of the group to say each number as you point to it.
- Write the word *set* on the chalkboard. Explain that the numbers make a set of data. **Which is the greatest number in the set?** *28* **Which is the smallest number?** *3* Have a volunteer use 28 and 3 to write and solve a subtraction sentence on the chalkboard. *28 – 3 = 25* Write the word *range* on the chalkboard. Explain that the difference between the greatest and smallest numbers in a set is called the range.
- Ask which number appears more than the other numbers in the set. *9* Write *mode* on the chalkboard. Explain that the number that occurs most often in a set is called the mode.
- Repeat with a new set of numbers, having students identify the *set*, *mode*, and *range*.

Activity Page 8-B

Name _____   Date _____

Using Tally Chart Data to Make a Bar Graph

Finish the bar graph. Write the title and subjects.

Fill in the correct number of spaces on each bar to show each vote. Look at the tally chart to see how many students voted for each subject.

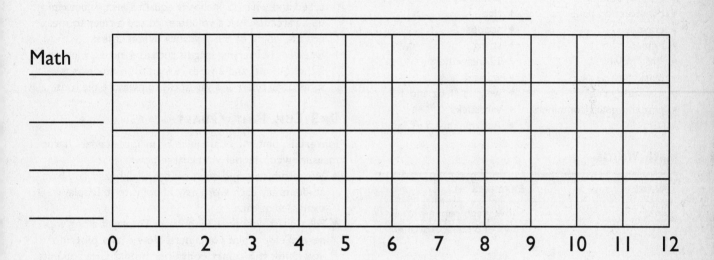

CHAPTER 9 Measurement

Objectives

- estimate and measure length in inches and feet
- estimate and measure length in inches, feet, and yards
- estimate and measure capacity in cups, pints, and quarts
- estimate and measure weight in ounces and pounds
- measure the perimeter of objects
- find the area of figures
- use a map to solve a problem

Cluster A Materials

- balance scale
- construction paper
- crayons
- funnel
- large bowls
- masking tape
- measuring cup
- pint and quart containers
- plastic zipper-lock bags
- rice
- scoops
- string
- 12-inch rulers
- water
- weights (1 oz and 1 lb)
- yardsticks
- Activity Page 9-A

Math Words

Words	Examples
area	Show graph paper with 6 rows of 6 squares shaded in.
foot [ft]	Show a 1-**foot** length of string.
inch [in.]	Show a 1-**inch** length of string.
length	Show a 6-inch **length** of string and tell students the **length**.
perimeter	Show a sheet of drawing paper with the length of each side marked.
yard [yd]	Show a **yard**-long line on the chalkboard.

Teaching Strategies See pp. v–vi for teaching tips on working with ELL students.

9•1 INCH AND FEET

Materials: inch rulers, varying lengths of string
- Display a ruler, explaining that each unit is an inch. Draw lines of varying lengths up to 2 feet on the chalk-board, including a 1-inch and a 12-inch line. Have students use a ruler to measure the lines. Explain that 12 inches equals 1 foot.
- Have students work in pairs. Give each partner a length of string between 2 and 24 inches. Have students estimate the length, tell their partners, and then measure to check.

9•2 INCHES, FEET, AND YARDS

Materials: 12-inch rulers, yardsticks
- Display a 12-inch ruler. Have students tell what a unit is called and what 12 inches is equal to. *inch; 1 foot* Hold up a yardstick. Ask a volunteer to use a ruler to measure the length of the yardstick in feet. *3 feet*
- Draw lines of varying lengths such as 4 inches, 9 inches, 12 inches (1 foot), and 2 yards (6 feet). Have students take turns using rulers and yardsticks to measure the lines.

9•3 CUP, PINT, QUART

Materials: pint and quart juice or milk containers, 1-cup measuring cup, funnel, water, large bowl
- Write *cup, pint,* and *quart* on the chalkboard, and have students say each word as you point to it. Display examples of each.
- Fill a quart container with water. Display it along with several empty pint containers. **How many pints do you think this quart container holds?** Give students time to answer. Then, have students count aloud as a volunteer pours the water into 2 empty pint containers. Write *1 quart = 2 pints* on the chalkboard.
- Display 1 of the pint containers of water and a measuring cup. **How many cups do you think this pint container holds?** Give students time to answer. Then, have students count aloud as a volunteer empties the water into a measuring cup. Write *1 pint = 2 cups* on the chalkboard.

9•4 OUNCE AND POUND

Materials: balance scales, 1 lb and 1 oz weights, plastic zipper lock bags, rice, bowl, scoops
- Write *pound* and *ounce* on the chalkboard. Have students point to each word as you say it. Then, have students feel a 1-lb weight and a 1-oz weight. **Which is heavier?** *pound* Use a balance scale, sixteen 1-oz weights, and a 1-lb weight to demonstrate that 16 ounces equals 1 pound.
- Have students work in pairs. Tell partners to fill a plastic bag with rice, stopping when they think they have a

pound, and then check their estimates with a balance scale and 1-lb weight.

9•5 PERIMETER

Materials: Activity Page 9-A
- Invite students to play "Follow the Leader." Have them form a line behind you. Starting at one corner, walk along each wall around the room. Count the steps aloud. When students have reached the starting point, explain that they have just walked the perimeter of the room, or the distance around it.
- Distribute activity page 9-A. Have each student create a figure by connecting dots across or down but not diagonally. Tell students that the distance across or down between each dot is 1 inch. To find the perimeter, have students count. Have each student display his or her figure, telling what the perimeter is. (Save activity pages for the next activity.)

9•6 AREA

Materials: completed activity pages from 9•5, crayons
- Display a completed activity page 9-A. Remind students that the perimeter of a figure is the distance around it.

Then write the word area on the chalkboard. Explain that the area of a figure is the number of square units it takes to cover it.
- Using the activity page, demonstrate how to connect the dots within the figure to make squares. Have students do the same. Then, have students color each square of the figure. **How do you think you can find the area of your figure?** *count the colored squares* Have students find the area of their figures. Invite students to share the results.

9•7 READING FOR MATH: USE MAPS

Materials: masking tape, construction-paper circles, rulers
- Make a tabletop map. Use masking tape to make the paths between locations and a numbered or lettered circle taped to each location. As students look at the map, point out that there is more than one path to get from one place to another.
- **How many different paths can you take to get from A to 3? Which path do you think is the shortest? How can you use your ruler to find out?** *measure and compare each path* (Save the tabletop map to use with activity 9•8 in Cluster B.)

Name _____ Date _____

Exploring Perimeter

Connect the dots → and ↓ to make a figure.

Then find the perimeter.

CLUSTER B, PAGES 325-341

Objectives

- use the Guess and Check strategy to solve problems
- measure length in centimeters
- estimate and measure weight in kilograms
- estimate and measure capacity in liters
- measure temperature in degrees Celsius and Fahrenheit
- determine the appropriate tool to use to measure weight, capacity, temperature, and length

Cluster B Materials

- 12-inch rulers
- balance scales
- bowl
- centimeter rulers
- containers (variety of sizes)
- crayons
- map from 9•7
- meter stick
- plastic zipper-lock bags
- rice
- scoops
- string
- string
- water
- weights (1 g and 1 kg)
- Activity Page 9-B

Math Words

Words	Examples
centimeter (cm)	Show 1 cm on a **centimeter** ruler.
meter (m)	Show a 1-**meter** length of string.
temperature	Have something cold and something warm for students to touch.

Teaching Strategies See pp. v–vi for teaching tips on working with ELL students.

9•8 PROBLEM SOLVING STRATEGY: GUESS AND CHECK

Materials: tabletop map from 9•7, rulers

- Have students look at the tabletop map. **How long do you think the path from A to 3 is?** As students share their guesses or estimates, record them on the chalkboard. **How can you find out if your guesses or estimates are correct?** *measure with a ruler* Have a volunteer measure the path. Then, have students decide which of their guesses or estimates makes sense. Afterward, explain that they have used the strategy Guess and Check to solve the problem.

9•9 CENTIMETER AND METER

Materials: centimeter rulers, meter stick

- Write *centimeter* on the chalkboard. Have students read the word. Give each student a centimeter ruler. **Why do you think it is called a centimeter ruler?** *Each unit is a centimeter.*
- Draw lines of varying lengths on the chalkboard between 1 and 15 centimeters. Have students take turns measuring the lines.
- Then, draw a 100-cm line on the chalkboard. Have a volunteer use a meter stick to measure the line. **How many centimeters long is the line?** *100 cm* Point out that the long ruler is 1 meter long, or 100 centimeters, and is called a meter stick. Write *100 centimeters = 1 meter* on the chalkboard.

9•10 GRAM AND KILOGRAM

Materials: balance scales, 1-g and 1-kg weights, plastic zipper-lock bags, rice, bowl, scoops

- Write *gram* and *kilogram* on the chalkboard. Have students point to each word as you say it. Then, have students feel a 1-g weight and a 1-kg weight. Ask which is heavier. *kilogram* Put a 1-kg weight on one side of a balance scale. Tell students that it would take 1,000 1-g weights to equal 1 kilogram.
- Have pairs of students fill a bag with rice, stopping when they think they have a kilogram, and then check their estimates with a balance scale and 1-kg weight.

9•10 LITER

Materials: 1-liter container; containers with a capacity of more than a liter, less than a liter, and a liter; water; funnel bowl

- Write *liter* on the chalkboard. Have students read the word. Display a 1-liter container. Tell students that it holds 1 liter.
- Fill the other containers. **Do you think this container holds more than a liter, less than a liter, or a liter?** Have students record their guesses. Have students check their guesses. Repeat with the remaining containers.

9•11 TEMPERATURE

Materials: crayons, Celsius and Fahrenheit thermometers, containers of ice water and very warm water, Activity Page 9-B

- Write *temperature, degrees Celsius, °C, degrees Fahrenheit,* and *°F* on the chalkboard.
- Have students give examples of things that are warm, hot, cool, and cold. Explain that how hot or cold some-

thing is, or temperature, can be measured in degrees Celsius and Fahrenheit.

- Have students form groups. Provide each with the two types of thermometers, containers of ice water and very warm water. Have students place both thermometers in the warm water first. After a minute, have them read the temperatures. Then, have students record the results on their worksheets. Repeat with the ice water. Encourage groups to share their results and observations. **Do the numbers go up or down when the water is cold or cool?** *down* **Do the numbers go up or down when the water is hot or warm?** *up*

9•11 MEASUREMENT TOOLS

Materials: scale measuring cup, ruler, thermometer, items that can be measured in some way by the tools

- As you display a tool, have students identify it. **What do you measure with a scale (thermometer, measuring cup, ruler)?** *weight (temperature, how much something holds, length)*
- On a table, display the gathered items. Have students in turn choose an object, such as a wooden block. **What tool can you use to find out if it is more than a pound or kilogram?** *scale* **What tool can use to find out it is 4 inches long?** *ruler* Then, have students demonstrate how to measure the block. Repeat with the other items.

Activity Page 9-B

Name _____ Date _____

Measuring, Reading, and Writing Temperatures

Put the thermometers in the warm water.

After a minute, read the temperatures.

Draw what you see. Write the temperatures.

Repeat with the cold water.

1. Warm Water

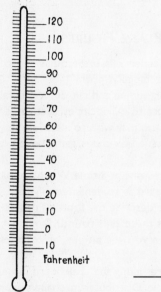

_____ °F   _____ °C

2. Cold Water

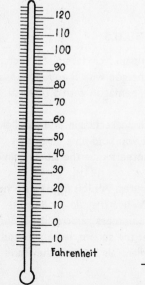

_____ °F   _____ °C

CHAPTER 10 Geometry

Objectives

- identify cone, cube, cylinder, pyramid, rectangular prism, sphere
- identify the shapes of faces of solid figures
- identify quadrilateral, parallelogram, and pentagon
- combine figures to make a hexagon, a trapezoid, and other figures
- solve math problems by making decisions

Cluster A Materials

- construction paper
- crayons
- drawing paper
- index cards
- models of solid figures
- paste
- pattern blocks
- scissors
- Activity Page 10-A

Math Words

Words	Examples
angle	Attach a label to a plane figure with an arrow pointing to one of its **angles**.
edge	Attach a label to a solid with an arrow pointing to an **edge**.
face	Attach a label to one **face** of a solid.
side	Attach a label to a plane with an arrow pointing to a **side**.
vertex	Attach a label to a plane figure with an arrow pointing to a **vertex**. **yard [yd]** Show a **yard**-long line on the chalkboard.

Teaching Strategies See pp. v–vi for teaching tips on working with ELL students.

10•1 SOLID FIGURES

Materials: index cards; models of a cone, cube, cylinder, pyramid, rectangular prism, sphere

- Use index cards to make labels for the solid figures. Arrange figures and labels on a table. As you point to a figure, have students read the label. Then hold up the figure and point out the faces, edges, and vertices.
- Remove the labels and distribute among students. Hold up a figure. Ask the student with the label to come forward and answer questions such as the following: **Does this figure have faces? How many? Can the figure roll? How many edges does it have? Where are the vertices?**
- As a variation, tell students you are thinking of a figure. Have them guess what it is by asking yes/no questions such as the following: **Does it come to a point? Can it roll? Does it have 6 faces? Does it have 12 edges? Does it have any vertices?**

10•2 SOLID AND PLANE FIGURES

Materials: construction paper; scissors; models of a cone, cube, cylinder, pyramid, rectangular prism

- On construction paper, outline and cut out the different faces of each solid figure to make circles, rectangles, squares, and triangles. You may wish to include classroom items such as tissue box cubes, game boxes, cans, and so on.
- Display the plane figures one at a time. Write the name of each on the chalkboard as students identify it. Encourage students to describe the figures. Prompt with questions such as these: **Is it round? Does it have sides? How many? Do you see angles, or corners? How many?**
- Arrange the solid figures along the chalkboard ledge, window sill, and/or table. Distribute the shapes, explaining how you made them. Have students take turns examining the solids to determine which one was used to make their plane figure.

10•3 MORE PLANE FIGURES

Materials: large construction-paper circle, square, rectangle, parallelogram, triangle, pentagon with 5 equal sides, pentagon shaped like a house, pentagon with 5 unequal sides; a label for each figure

- Tape the square, triangle, circle, rectangle, and parallelogram to the chalkboard. As you hold up a label, have students read it. Have volunteers tape the labels below the matching figures.
- Have students study the figures. **Which figures do not belong?** *circle and triangle* **Why?** *They do not have 4 sides and 4 corners.* Have volunteers remove the 2 figures and labels. Explain that the square, rectangle, and parallelogram are all quadrilaterals because they have 4

sides and 4 angles, or corners. Write *quadrilaterals* on the chalkboard.

- Follow a similar procedure to introduce the pentagon, using a parallelogram, triangle, and the 3 pentagons.

10•4 MAKE FIGURES

Materials: large construction-paper hexagon and trapezoid, scissors, crayons, drawing paper, paste, Activity Page 10-A

- Write the words *hexagon* and *trapezoid* on the chalkboard and read them aloud. Display the figures and identify them. Have volunteers tape each figure below its label. Then, continue by counting the sides and angles of each figure with students.
- Remove the hexagon. Tell students you can cut the hexagon to make 2 figures. Demonstrate, by cutting the hexagon to make 2 trapezoids. Repeat with the trapezoid, cutting at a diagonal to make a triangle and a parallelogram.

- Distribute activity pages and art materials. Give the following directions, one at a time: Color and cut out each figure. Cut out the labels. Match the figures and labels. Cut each figure along the dashed line. Tell what figures you get. Mix up the labels and figures. Now, put the parts back together to make the figures you started with. Paste the figures and labels to your paper.

10•5 READING FOR MATH: MAKE DECISIONS

Materials: pattern blocks

- Have students work in pairs and small groups to make a clown figure using different pattern blocks. Give them 5 minutes to complete the task.
- Ask partners and groups which pattern block or blocks they used to make the head, hat, arms, body, and so on and to explain why they made the choices they did.

Activity Page 10-A

Name _____ Date _____

Exploring Plane Figures

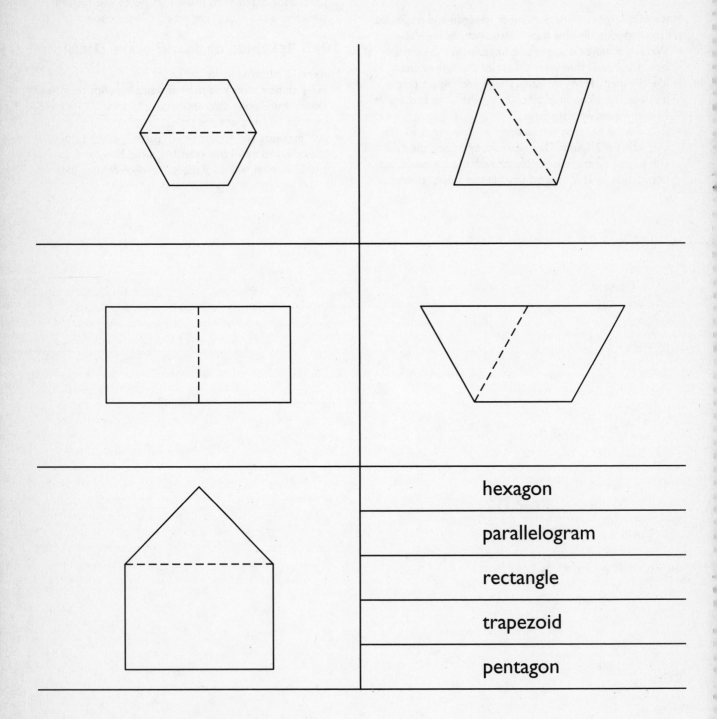

hexagon

parallelogram

rectangle

trapezoid

pentagon

Objectives

- use pattern blocks to act out solutions to problems
- identify congruent plane figures
- identify lines of symmetry

Cluster B Materials

- construction paper
- crayons
- black marker
- pattern blocks
- scissors
- Activity Page 10-B

Math Words

Words	Examples
congruent	Show examples of figures with the same shape and size.
line of symmetry	Show examples of figures with and without **lines of symmetry**.

Teaching Strategies See pp. v–vi for teaching tips on working with ELL students.

10•6 PROBLEM SOLVING STRATEGY: ACT IT OUT

Materials: 7 pattern-block triangles, 1 trapezoid, and 1 parallelogram for each student pair; construction-paper triangles

- In advance, size triangles so that 4 pattern-block triangles and/or 1 pattern-block parallelogram and 2 triangles and/or 1 trapezoid and 1 triangle can be used to make the figure.
- Distribute a paper triangle and pattern blocks. Tell students you want to find a way to use the pattern blocks to make a triangle that is exactly the same size as the paper triangle. Give partners several minutes to complete the task.
- Encourage partners to share their results, telling which figures they used and how many of each. Afterward, tell students they used the Act It Out strategy to help solve the problem.

10•7 CONGRUENT FIGURES

Materials: construction-paper circles, squares, triangles, rectangles, trapezoids, parallelograms of different sizes (at least 2 of each shape must be congruent)

- Have students organize themselves into groups of 5. Give each group member a paper shape. Make sure that 2 shapes are congruent. Then, have group members compare their shapes and identify the 2 that are exactly the same size and shape. Repeat several more times.
- Have group members with identical shapes stand together in front of the room. Write the word *congruent* on the chalkboard. Tell students that each pair of shapes is congruent. Then, challenge students to define the word *congruent. having the same size and shape.*

10•8 SYMMETRY

Materials: 2 large construction-paper hearts, black marker, scissors, crayons, Activity Page 10-B

- Use the marker to draw a line of symmetry on one heart and a diagonal line across the other. Tell students you will cut along each line. **Which heart do you think will have 2 parts that match exactly when I am finished?** Have students share their ideas. Then, cut out the hearts and show the results. Write *line of symmetry* on the chalkboard and tape the 2 matching parts to the chalkboard. Point to the line, explaining that this heart has a line of symmetry because the 2 parts match. Next, show the other heart, pointing out that it does not have a line of symmetry.
- Distribute activity pages. Have students work in pairs. Point out the dark line and say it is a line of symmetry. Have one partner begin by coloring in squares above the line to create a pattern. Then, have the other partner color in squares below the line, copying the pattern so that both parts will match exactly when cut or folded along the line. Have partners check by cutting or folding to see if the two parts match. Then repeat, having the partner who copied the pattern now create one.

Activity Page 10-B

Name _____ Date _____

Making Shapes That Match

Draw a figure with 2 parts that match exactly.
Take turns with your partner.
Color in squares above the line to start.
Color in squares below the line to finish.
Cut out the shape. Then fold or cut along the line.

Do both parts match?

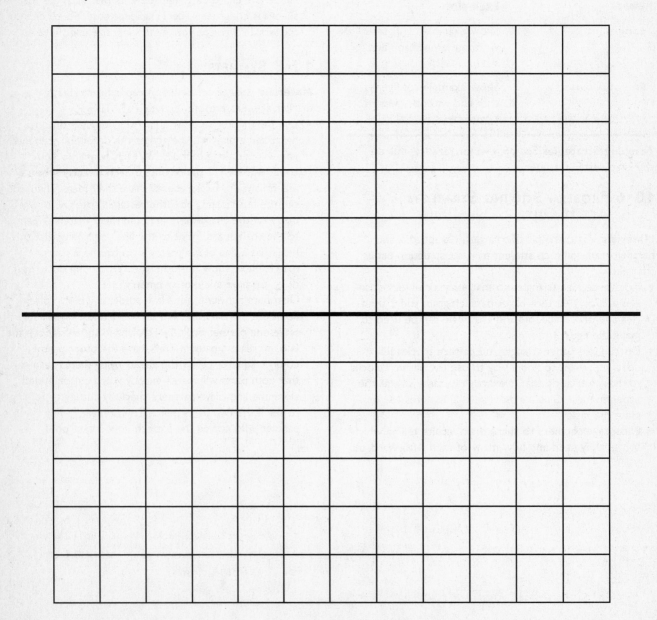

CHAPTER 11 Fractions and Probability

CLUSTER A, PAGES 385-396

Objectives

- understand and identify halves, fourths, and eighths
- understand and identify thirds, sixths, and twelfths
- understand and identify more than one equal part of a whole
- compare fractions
- use data in a story problem to make predictions

Cluster A Materials

- $8\frac{1}{2}$" x 11" paper
- construction paper
- crayons
- large envelopes
- large paper plates
- scissors
- tagchalkboard
- Activity Page 11-A

Math Words

Words	Examples
eighths	Show a paper plate divided into **eighths**.
fourths	Show a paper plate divided into **fourths**.
fraction	$\frac{1}{2}$ $\frac{1}{3}$ $\frac{1}{4}$
halves	Show a paper plate divided into **halves**.
sixths	Show a paper plate divided into **sixths**.
thirds	Show a paper plate divided into **thirds**.
twelfths	Show a paper plate divided into **twelfths**.

Teaching Strategies See pp. v–vi for teaching tips on working with ELL students.

11•1 HALVES, FOURTHS, AND EIGHTHS

Materials: 3 sheets of $8\frac{1}{2}$" x 11" paper per student, crayons (Glossy finish pages from department store fliers and magazines work well with this and the next activity.)

- Distribute paper to students. Model how to fold a sheet of paper into 2 equal parts. Have students do the same. **Are the parts equal?** *yes* **How many equal parts are there?** *2*

- Write *halves* on the chalkboard. Have students say the word. Explain that the 2 equal parts they made by folding the paper are called halves. Next, have students color in 1 part. Write *one half* and $\frac{1}{2}$ on the chalkboard. Explain that 1 of 2 equal parts is one half.

- Follow a similar procedure to illustrate fourths and eighths. To show fourths, fold the paper in half twice. To show eighths, fold the paper in half 3 times.

11•2 THIRDS, SIXTHS, AND TWELFTHS

Materials: 3 sheets of $8\frac{1}{2}$" x 11" paper per student, crayons

Distribute paper to students. Demonstrate how to fold a sheet of paper into 3 equal parts. Have students do the same. **Are the parts equal?** *yes* **How many equal parts are there?** *3*

- Write *thirds* on the chalkboard. Have students say the word. Explain that the 3 equal parts they made by folding the paper are called thirds . Next, have students color in 1 part. Write *one third* and $\frac{1}{3}$ on the chalkboard. Explain that 1 of 3 equal parts is one third.

- Follow a similar procedure to illustrate sixths and eighths. To show sixths, fold the paper in thirds and then in half. To show twelfths, fold the paper in thirds and then in half twice.

11•3 MORE FRACTIONS

Materials: 5 large tagboard rectangles, squares, or circles; marker; construction paper; scissors; large envelopes

- In advance, divide each tagboard shape into thirds, fourths, sixths, eighths, or twelfths. Cut the following fractional parts to fit the corresponding shapes: $\frac{1}{4}$, $\frac{2}{4}$, $\frac{3}{4}$, $\frac{1}{3}$, $\frac{2}{3}$, $\frac{1}{6}-\frac{5}{6}$, $\frac{1}{8}-\frac{7}{8}$, $\frac{1}{12}-\frac{11}{12}$. Put the parts into individual envelopes labeled *thirds, fourths, sixths, eighths,* and *twelfths*.

- Display the "sixths" shape, for example. Ask a student to pick a fractional part from the envelope, such as $\frac{5}{6}$, and cover that part of the shape. Ask how the shape is divided and what part is now covered. *sixths;* $\frac{5}{6}$ Remove the shape. Repeat, calling on a new student. Then, have students work in pairs or small groups to determine fractions of other shapes.

11•4 COMPARE FRACTIONS

Materials: crayons, scissors, Activity Page 11-A
- Distribute the activity page. Have students look at the first rectangle and count the number of equal parts. Have them color in 1 part with a yellow crayon and write the fraction for the shaded part with a black crayon. $\frac{1}{2}$ Repeat the procedure with fourths, eighths, thirds, sixths, and twelfths. Then, have students cut out each rectangle and the fractional parts they colored.
- Ask students to find the 2 parts that show, for example, one half and one eighth and place them side by side on their desks. **Which fraction is greater (less), $\frac{1}{8}$ or $\frac{1}{2}$?** $\frac{1}{2}$ Then, have students point to or hold up the correct fractional part. Continue by asking students to find other pairs of fractional parts and compare them.

11•5 READING FOR MATH: MAKING PREDICTIONS

Materials: large and small paper plates, scissors
- Draw a line to show one fourth of a wedge on the large plate and one third of a wedge on the small plate.
- Give each pair of students a large plate, a small plate, and 2 pairs of scissors. Explain that you will read a story problem with 2 characters. Ask the partner with the small plate to be Max and the partner with the large plate Sam.
- Read the following aloud: **Max and Sam each baked an apple pie. Max ate $\frac{1}{3}$ of his pie. Sam ate only $\frac{1}{4}$ of his.** Have "Max" and "Sam" cut out the part they each ate. Ask "Max" how much of his pie is left? $\frac{2}{3}$ Ask "Sam" how much of his pie is left. $\frac{3}{4}$ Continue the story: **Sam says he ate more than Max. Is this possible?** yes **How?** Have "Max" and "Sam" compare the two wedges and size of the pies they made.

Activity Page 11-A

Name _____   Date _____

Exploring Fractions

CLUSTER B, PAGES 399-408

Objectives

- draw a picture to solve problems
- identify fractions of groups
- find fractions of groups
- find the most likely and the least likely outcomes
- make predictions

Cluster B Materials

- 2-color counters
- construction paper (red, yellow)
- crayons, including red and yellow
- drawing paper
- envelopes
- paper lunch bags
- play dimes and pennies
- scissors
- index cards
- Activity Page 11-B

Teaching Strategies See pp. v–vi for teaching tips on working with ELL students.

11•6 PROBLEM SOLVING STRATEGY: DRAW A PICTURE

Materials: drawing paper, crayons
- Review the Four-Step Process: Read, Plan, Solve, Check.
- Write the following problem on the chalkboard: **Fran and Ann were straightening Ann's dresser. The dresser has 6 drawers. Fran straightened 2 drawers, and Ann straightened 1 drawer. What fraction of the dresser did they straighten?** Have students read and restate the problem. Explain that they will draw a picture to solve it.
- **How can you show the dresser?** *by drawing a rectangle* **How will you divide the dresser?** *into 6 equal drawers* **How will you show the number of drawers Fran and Ann straightened?** *color in 3 drawers* **How will you write the fraction to show what part the children straightened?** $\frac{3}{6}$ Help students as needed. Refer to lesson 11•3. You may also wish to have students tell/write what fraction of the dresser is left. $\frac{3}{6}$

11•7 FRACTIONS OF A GROUP

Materials: small red and yellow construction-paper squares (or connecting cubes), index cards with a line drawn across the middle to make fraction templates, index cards cut in half for number cards, envelopes, red and yellow crayons, Activity Page 11-B
- Give each student an envelope with a combination of 6, 8, or 12 red and yellow squares, a fraction template, and 3 blank index cards.
- Have students arrange the squares in a row, putting the red squares first. **How many squares are red? How many squares are yellow? How many squares do**
you have in all? Have students write each number on a blank card.
- Then, have students use the fraction card and number cards to show what fraction of their squares are red and yellow. Have students draw and record the results on their activity pages. Students can then trade envelopes and follow the same procedure 2 more times.

11•8 MORE FRACTIONS OF A GROUP

Materials: 2-color counters
- Give each student 2-color counters. Tell students to do the following: **Count out 8 counters. Arrange the counters in 2 rows of 4 on your paper. Make all the counters in the top row red. Make all the counters in the bottom row yellow. Draw a line between the 2 rows.**
- **How many equal parts did you make?** *2* **What fraction of the parts are red?** $\frac{1}{2}$ Repeat the procedure, having students model and identify other fractions of groups.

11•9 MOST LIKELY AND LEAST LIKELY OUTCOMES

Materials: play dimes and pennies, paper lunch bags
- Give pairs of students a bag with 8 dimes and 2 pennies. Have partners remove the coins from the bag, tell how many of each they have, put the coins back in the bag, and shake it up. **Which coin are you most likely to pick?** *dime* **Why do you think so?** *There are more dimes than pennies.* **Which coin are you least likely to pick?** *penny* **Why do you think so?** *There are only 2 pennies and 8 dimes.*
- Have partners take turns picking a coin from the bag without looking to confirm their conclusions. You may wish to have students increase the number of pennies and decrease the number of dimes and repeat.

11•10 MAKE PREDICTIONS

Materials: play dimes and pennies, paper lunch bags
- Give pairs of students a bag of coins with combinations such as the following: 1 dime/14 pennies, 2 dimes/13 pennies, 3 dimes/ 12 pennies, 4 dimes/10 pennies, 5 dimes/10 pennies.
- Have partners first count how many coins they have in all and how many they have of each coin. **Which coin do you think you will pick most often if you pick 10 times? Why do you think so?** Have partners jot down their guesses, or predictions, and then take turns picking a coin without looking, 10 times each. As one partner picks, have the other partner record the results.
- After partners complete their turns, invite them to share their results with the class.

Activity Page 11-B

Name _____ Date _____

Writing Fractions

Draw and color the squares each time	Write the fraction for the red part.	Write the fraction for the yellow part.
	☐/☐	☐/☐
	☐/☐	☐/☐
	☐/☐	☐/☐

CHAPTER 12 Place Value to 1, 000

Objectives

- make groups of 100
- identify hundreds, tens, and ones to show 3-digit numbers
- understand the value of each digit in a 3-digit number
- count on or back by hundreds
- read and write 3-digit numbers
- write the expanded form of 3-digit numbers
- identify and use clues to solve problems

Cluster A Materials

- connecting cubes (red and yellow)
- index cards
- hundreds flats
- scissors
- tagboard
- tens rods
- unit cubes
- Activity Page 12-A

Math Words

Words	Examples
digits	4 2 5
	means 4 hundreds means 2 tens means 5 ones
hundred	Show a hundred model.
place value	Show a place value chart that includes ones, tens, and hundreds.

Teaching Strategies See pp. v–vi for teaching tips on working with ELL students.

12•1 HUNDREDS

Materials: tagchalkboard cut into 11" x 2" strips, stickers (or $\frac{3}{4}$" construction-paper squares, paste, and crayons)
- Distribute tagchalkboard strips and stickers to small groups of students to make a total of 9 groups. **If each group makes exactly 10 strips with 10 stickers on each, how many groups of hundreds will we have in all?** As each group completes the task, have them count out 10 strips in exchange for 1 hundreds model. **How many ones make 1 ten?** *10 ones* **How many tens**

make 1 hundred? *10 tens* **How many ones make 1 hundred?** *100 ones*
- Have each group hold up its hundred model in turn as everyone counts aloud **1 group of hundred, 2 groups of hundred, 3 groups of hundred,** and so on. Write

_____ groups of hundred on the chalkboard. Have a volunteer write the number in the blank. Write

_____ hundreds = _____ in all; have students tell what numbers belong in each blank based on the results.

12•2 HUNDREDS, TENS, AND ONES

Materials: ones cubes, tens rods, hundreds flats; index cards
- Make sets of ones, tens, and hundreds cards. Write 1-9 ones, tens, or hundreds on each; for example: 2 ones, 4 tens, 5 hundreds. Have students work in groups of 3. Distribute and a one, ten, and hundred card to each group.
- Have each group member take a card and show the number of ones, tens, or hundreds to make a 3-digit number. Have one member from each group say the number they showed and then write it on the chalkboard. Repeat 2 more times with a different set of numbers so each group member has the opportunity to say and record a number.

12•3 MORE HUNDREDS, TENS, AND ONES

Materials: index cards cut in half
- Distribute 9 blank cards to each student. Have students write a number from 1-9 on each card.
- Call out a 3-digit number such as 438. Give students time to show the number with their number cards. Then, write the number on the chalkboard and have students check to see if their number matches the one you wrote.
- Tell students to hold up the correct card to answer each of these questions: **What is the digit in the tens place? What is the digit in the hundreds place? What is the digit in the ones place?** Point to the correct digit on the chalkboard.

12•4 COUNTING ON OR BACK BY HUNDREDS

Materials: ones cubes, tens rods, hundreds flats
- Have students work in pairs. Write a 3-digit number, such as 456, on the chalkboard. Have one partner show and

say the number. Ask the other partner to add 100 to the model and say the new number. Write *556* on the chalkboard under the first number. Next, have each partner remove 100 from the model and say the new number. Write *356* on the chalkboard above the first number.

- Point to 456. **What is 100 more than 456?** *556* **What is 100 less than 456?** *356* Then, continue by asking to name 100 more than 556, 400 less than 656, 100 less than 256, and so on until you have a column of numbers between 56 and 956.

12•5 NUMBERS TO 1,000

Materials: tagchalkboard cards for 3-digit numbers, number words, and hundreds/tens/ones frames

- For each 3-digit number, make a word card, a number card, and a place value frame with the hundreds, tens, and ones filled in.
- Have students form 2 lines, 1 on each side of the room. Distribute word cards to students in one line and number cards to students in the other line. Hold up a place value card. Have students with the matching number and word cards step forward, read their cards, and place them along the chalkboard ledge along with your card. Continue until all cards are matched.

12•6 EXPANDED FORM

Materials: scissors, Activity Page 12-A

- Write *expanded form* on the chalkboard. Remind students that they can show a number in different ways

and that one way is called expanded form. Have students read the words.

- Distribute activity pages. Have students cut apart the activity page to make 27 cards. As you call out a set of numbers, such as 500 +/ 40 +/ 7 to make a 3-digit number, give students time to find and arrange the cards on their desk. Explain that this is the expanded form of the number 547. To make the number, have students slide the 40 + card to the left until the 4 is in the tens place and slide the 7 card to the left until it is in the ones place. Ask students to repeat the number. Have a volunteer write the number on the chalkboard.
- Continue until all the number sections have been used. Then have student volunteers suggest more numbers for the class to expand.

12•7 READING FOR MATH: PROBLEM AND SOLUTIONS

Materials: 10 yellow and 6 red connecting cubes

- Use 4 red and 6 yellow cubes to begin the following pattern: red, yellow, yellow. Display the pattern horizontally. Say: **I am making a cube train. I have 10 yellow cubes and 6 red ones.**
- **How many cubes in all will I use?** *16* **What is the pattern of my cube train?** *red, yellow, yellow* **What color is the last cube that I will add to my train?** *red* Point out that students used clues to solve problems. Encourage students to identify them. *the cube train you started, the information telling how many of each cube you planned to use*

Name _____ Date _____

Showing Numbers Two Ways (Expanded Form)

Cut out the cards. Make expanded numbers.
Then, move the cards together to show the 3-digit
number.

900 +	90 +	9
800 +	80 +	8
700 +	70 +	7
600 +	60 +	6
500 +	50 +	5
400 +	40 +	4
300 +	30 +	3
200 +	20 +	2
100 +	10 +	1

Objectives

- identify and use a pattern to solve problems
- compare 3-digit numbers
- order 3-digit numbers
- describe and extend number patterns

Cluster B Materials

- 3-digit number cards
- <, >, and = signs
- index cards (4" x 6")
- large and small paper clips
- number cubes
- Activity Page 12-B

Key Concepts See pp. xx for teaching strategies for working with ELL students.

12•8 PROBLEM SOLVING STRATEGY: FIND A PATTERN

Materials: large and small paper clips

- Make and distribute chains that are 7 paper-clips long to show the following pattern: short, short, short, long.
- Review the Four-Step Process: Read, Plan, Solve, Check.
- Read aloud the following problem: **Clara is making a paper clip necklace. She has used 7 paper clips so far. How will she complete the necklace?** Have students read and restate the problem. **What must you know before you can solve the problem?** *the pattern* **How can you figure out the pattern?** *by looking at the necklace* **When you try to figure out a pattern, what might you look for?** *color, size, shape, number* **Look at Clara's necklace. What pattern do you see?** *short, short, short, long* **What paper clip should Clara add next?** *a short one* Have students continue and complete the pattern.

12•9 COMPARE NUMBERS

Materials: <, >, and = signs; for each student pair: 3 number cubes with these numbers: 1–6; 3–8; 1–5, 9; Activity Page 12-B

- Have 2 volunteers face the group. Ask one volunteer to roll the number cubes and say the 3-digit number aloud as you write it on the chalkboard, for example, 328. Hold up the > sign, then write it on the chalkboard next to the number. Have the group think of a number that would make the comparison true. Have the second volunteer write the agreed-upon number on the chalkboard. Have the class read the comparison.
- Distribute activity pages and 3 number cubes to student pairs. Begin by using the same number as above. Have Partner A write the number under "Partner A" on the first line in the first row. Call attention to the

greater than sign and the direction line in the box, "Change the tens." **What number could you write that is greater than 328 but differs only by the tens?** *338, 348, 358, and so on* Have Partner B write a number on the second line to complete the comparison: 328 > _____ .

- Have partners reverse roles. Partner B now rolls the 3 cubes to make a new 3-digit number and records it under "Partner B" in the first row. Partner A reads the sign and directions and writes a number to complete the comparison. Partners continue taking turns to complete the page.

12•10 ORDER NUMBERS

Materials: 4" x 6" index cards

- Prepare sets of index cards as follows: write one 3-digit number on each card so that the set consists of 6 numbers in sequence, for example, 362 to 367.
- Randomly distribute a set of cards to a small group of students. At your signal, have group members arrange themselves in order according to the numbers that they hold, going from least to greatest in value and from right to left when facing the class.
- Have students read the numbers aloud, making sure they are in order. Then, ask questions such as **What comes just before 366?** *365* **What comes between 362 and 364?** *363* **What comes just after 365?** *366* Hold up 2 blank cards. **What numbers come just before 362 and just after 367?** *361; 368* Record the numbers. Give the cards to 2 volunteers and have them take their places in line.
- Repeat with other groups of students and number sequences.

12•11 NUMBER PATTERNS

Materials: 4" x 6" index cards

- Prepare sets of cards consisting of five 3-digit numbers to illustrate counting by hundreds, tens, and ones. For example: 210, 220, 230, 240, 250; 243, 343, 443, 543, 643; 261, 262, 263, 264, 265.
- Randomly distribute sets of cards to groups of students. Have groups arrange their cards in order from least to greatest, and then figure out the pattern. Remind students to check ones, tens, and hundreds. Then at your signal, have group members stand and hold the cards in order. Ask them to say the numbers on their cards and tell the pattern.
- Hold up 2 blank index cards. Ask students what number comes before the first number and after the last number. Record the numbers. Have each group add the numbers to the lineup.

Activity Page 12-B

Name _____ Date _____

Comparing Numbers

Take turns with a partner.

Roll 3 number cubes. Write the number on the first line.

Then have your partner write a number that is greater than or less than your number. Be sure to read the direction in the box!

Partner A	Partner B

Change the tens.

_____ > _____   _____ > _____

Change the ones.

_____ < _____   _____ < _____

Change the hundreds.

_____ > _____   _____ > _____

You and your partner choose.

◯ _____   ◯ _____

CHAPTER 13 Add and Subtract 3-Digit Numbers

CLUSTER A, PAGES 463-478

Objectives

- add hundreds by counting on
- use basic facts to add hundreds, tens, and ones
- decide whether regrouping is needed when adding
- add 3-digit numbers with and without regrouping
- estimate sums
- identify main idea and details in story problems

Cluster A Materials

- counters
- hundreds flats
- index cards
- masking tape
- ones cubes
- tens rods
- Activity Page 13-A

Math Words

Words	Examples
addend	125 + 231 = 356
hundreds	247
regroup	15 ones = 1 ten and 5 ones

Teaching Strategies See pp. v–vi for teaching tips on working with ELL students.

13•1 ADD HUNDREDS

Materials: masking tape
- Make a masking-tape number line for hundreds (0 to 1000) on the classroom floor. Mark numbers so they are about 12 inches apart.
- Ask a student to start on 400 and then jump ahead 3 hundreds. **What number did you land on?** *700* Ask the student to repeat the action, this time saying 500, 600, 700 as he or she jumps. **How can we show this as an addition sentence?** *400 + 300 = 700* Write the addition sentence.
- Call on pairs of students to illustrate problems such as 200 + 500, 600 + 400, 100 + 800. Ask one partner to follow your directions to jump and count aloud, while the other student writes the addition sentence on the chalkboard. Explain to students that they have been counting on to add hundreds. (Save the number line for use with activity 13•8.)

13•2 3-DIGIT ADDITION WITHOUT REGROUPING

Materials: ones cubes, tens rods, hundreds flats
- Distribute cubes, rods, and flats to pairs of students. Write *132 + 847* in vertical form on the chalkboard. Draw a line between the hundreds, tens, and ones. Have a student label the columns.
- Have each partner use cubes, rods, and flats to show an addend. **To solve the problem, do you add ones, tens, or hundreds first?** *ones* Have partners combine the ones and tell how many. *9 ones* **What will you add next?** *tens* Have partners combine the tens and tell how many. *7 tens* Repeat with the hundreds. *9 hundreds* Ask a volunteer to repeat the problem, say the sum, and write the answer on the chalkboard to complete the problem. *979*
- Repeat the activity with other 3-digit addition problems that do not require regrouping.

13•3 3-DIGIT ADDITION

Materials: ones cubes, tens rods, hundreds flats
- Distribute cubes, rods, and flats to pairs of students. Have one partner show 2 hundreds 6 tens 2 ones and the other partner show 3 hundreds 5 tens 3 ones. Have partners combine ones and tell how many. *5 ones* **Do you need to regroup?** *no* **Why not?** *There are only 5 ones* Have partners combine tens. **Do you need to regroup?** *yes* **Why?** *There are more than 9 tens.* **How do you regroup 11 tens?** *as 1 hundred 1 ten* Have partners regroup, combine the hundreds, and tell how many. *6 hundreds* Write 262 + 353 = 615 in vertical form on the chalkboard, showing the regrouping.
- Repeat the procedure with a problem that does not require regrouping, such as 432 + 257.

13•4 MORE 3-DIGIT ADDITION

Materials: ones cubes, tens rods, hundreds flats, index cards, Activity Page 13-A
- Write the following numbers on index cards: 479, 287, 365, 156, 278, 199, 367, 515, 458, 259, 346, 188. Distribute activity pages and other materials to pairs of students.
- Have one partner pick 2 cards and show the numbers with cubes, rods, and flats. Have the other partner write the numbers on the activity page to make an addition problem. As the one partner adds on the activity page, have the other partner use cubes, rods, and flats to

show each step. Before students begin, ask: **In what order will you add or combine models?** *one, tens, hundreds* **How will you know when to regroup?** *when the sum of ones or tens is more than 9* Have partners complete the first problem.
- Then, have partners switch roles and repeat.

13•5 ESTIMATE SUMS

Materials: masking tape, counters, Activity Page 13-A
- Distribute an activity page to each pair of students. Write 289 + 412 in vertical form on the chalkboard. Have one partner copy the problem onto the activity page and add. **Is your answer reasonable?** Give students time to answer.
- Have the other partner add the nearest hundreds to see. First, tape a strip of masking tape to each desk so partners can make a hundreds number line. Using counters, have the partner mark where 289 and 412 would be on the number line. **Is 289 nearer to 300 or to 200?** *300* **Is 412 nearer to 500 or to 400?** *400* Have the partner write 300 + 400 on the activity page and add. Have partners compare the 2 sums. **Are the sums close?** If students answer yes, explain that the sum of 289 + 412 is reasonable.

- Give partners 2 more problems. Have them take turns adding to find the sum and checking by finding and adding nearest hundreds.

13•6 READING FOR MATH: MAIN IDEA AND DETAILS

Materials: ones cubes, tens rods, hundreds flats
- Write the following on the chalkboard: **Shaida and Daniel collect cans of food for the Hillside Food Bank. Shaida collected 315 cans from her friends and neighbors. Daniel collected 297 cans from his class.**
- **What is the main idea?** *Children collect canned food for the food bank.* Have a volunteer underline the sentence that tells the main idea. **What do you want to find out?** *how many cans the children collected* **What details will help you?** *Shaida collected 315 cans; Daniel collected 297 cans.* Have a volunteer circle the two details.
- Have students use cubes, rods, and flats and/or paper and pencil to calculate how many cans of food the children collected. *612 cans* Ask a volunteer to write a number sentence on the chalkboard to show this.

Activity Page 13-A

Adding Hundreds, Tens, and Ones

Hundreds	Tens	Ones
☐	☐	
+		

Hundreds	Tens	Ones
☐	☐	
+		

Hundreds	Tens	Ones
☐	☐	
+		

Hundreds	Tens	Ones
☐	☐	
+		

Hundreds	Tens	Ones
☐	☐	
+		

Hundreds	Tens	Ones
☐	☐	
+		

CLUSTER B, PAGES 481-496

Objectives

- make a graph to solve a problem
- subtract hundreds by counting back
- use basic facts to subtract hundreds, tens, ones
- decide whether regrouping is needed when subtracting
- subtract 3-digit numbers with and without regrouping
- estimate differences
- add and subtract money amounts

Cluster B Materials

- counters
- crayons
- envelopes
- glue
- hundreds flats
- index cards in 2 different colors
- masking tape
- ones cubes
- play dollar bills and coins
- scissors
- tens rods
- Activity Page 13-B

Teaching Strategies See pp. v–vi for teaching tips on working with ELL students.

13•7 PROBLEM SOLVING STRATEGY: MAKE A GRAPH

Materials: scissors, glue, crayons, Activity Page 13-B

- Write this problem on the chalkboard: **Some children have a stamp collection. Luisa has 38 new flower stamps. Annie has 21 new bird stamps. Diego has 29 new famous people stamps. About how many new stamps do the children have in all?** Have students read the problem. **What do you know?** *how many new stamps each child has* **What do you want to find out?** *about how many stamps they have in all* **What strategies could you use to solve the problem?** *act it out, draw a picture* Tell students they can also make a graph to solve the problem.
- Distribute Activity Page 13-B. Work together. Have students cut out the graph parts, decide where each part belongs, and paste the parts in place. Next, have students color in spaces to show how many of each stamp the children have. To find about how many new stamps in all, help students round up or down to the nearest five and add. *about 90*

13•8 SUBTRACT HUNDREDS

Materials: masking-tape number line

- Use the masking-tape number line from activity 13•1. Ask a student to start on 800 and then jump back 5 hundreds. **What number did you land on?** *300* Have the student repeat the action, this time saying 700, 600, 500, 400, 300 as he or she jumps. **How can we show**

this as a subtraction sentence? *800 – 500 = 300* Write the sentence on the chalkboard.
- Call on pairs of students to illustrate problems such as 700 – 200, 600 – 400, 900 – 800. As one partner follows your directions to jump and count back aloud, have the other partner write the subtraction sentence on the chalkboard.

13•9 3-DIGIT SUBTRACTION WITHOUT REGROUPING

Materials: ones cubes, tens rods, hundreds flats

- Distribute materials to student pairs. Write 567 - 243 in vertical form on the chalkboard. Draw a line between hundreds, tens, and ones, and have a volunteer label the columns.
- Have partners use cubes, rods, and flats to show 567. **To subtract 243, do you start with ones, tens, or hundreds first?** *ones* Have partners remove 3 ones and tell how many are left. *4 ones* **What subtraction fact could you use?** *7 – 3 = 4* **What will you subtract next?** *tens* Have partners remove 4 tens and tell how many are left. *2 tens* **What subtraction fact could you use?** *6 – 4 = 2* Repeat with the hundreds. *3 hundreds; 5 – 2 = 3* Ask a volunteer to repeat the problem, state the difference, and write the answer on the chalkboard to complete the problem. *324*
- Repeat the activity with other 3-digit subtraction problems that do not require regrouping.

13•10 3-DIGIT SUBTRACTION

Materials: ones cubes, tens rods, hundreds flats

- Write the following on the chalkboard: 5 hundreds 6 tens 7 ones and 3 hundreds 7 tens 2 ones. Distribute cubes, rods, and flats to student pairs. Have one partner show 5 hundreds 6 tens 7 ones. Tell the other partner to subtract 3 hundreds 7 tens 2 ones.
- **To subtract 2 ones, do you need to regroup?** *no* **Why not?** *There are enough ones to subtract.* Have the partner remove 2 ones. **How many ones are left?** *5 ones* **To subtract 7 tens, do you need to regroup?** *yes* **Why?** *There aren't enough tens.* Have the partner regroup 1 hundred as 10 tens, combine them with the 6 tens, and then subtract 7 tens. **How many tens are left?** *9* Have the partner subtract 3 hundreds from the remaining 4 hundreds. How many hundreds are left? *1 hundred* Write 567 – 372 = 195 in vertical form on the chalkboard, showing the regrouping.
- Have partners repeat the activity with other problems.

13•11 MORE 3-DIGIT SUBTRACTION

Materials: ones cubes, tens rods, hundreds flats, index cards in 2 colors cut in half

- Write the following numbers on cards of one color: 643, 625, 742, 854, 912. Write these numbers on cards of a second color: 567, 486, 378, 399, 166. Distribute cubes, rods, flats, two sets of number cards, and paper to student pairs.
- Have one partner pick one card from each set of cards and write the numbers in vertical form on paper to make a subtraction problem. As the one partner subtracts on paper, have the other partner show use cubes, rods, and flats.
- Before students begin, ask **In what order will you subtract?** *ones, tens, hundreds* **How will you know when to regroup?** *when the number we subtract is more than the number we are subtracting from*
- Have partners switch roles and continue until all the cards are used.

13•12 ESTIMATE DIFFERENCES

Materials: masking tape, counters
- Write 638 − 419 in vertical form on the chalkboard. Have one partner copy the problem and subtract. **Is your answer reasonable?** Give students time to answer. Then, have their partner subtract the nearest hundreds to see.
- Tape a strip of masking tape to each desk. Have partners make a hundreds number line. Using counters, have one partner mark where 638 and 419 would be on the number line. **Is 638 nearer to 700 or to 600?** *600* **Is 419 nearer to 500 or to 400?** *400* Have the other partner write 600 − 400 and subtract. Have partners compare the 2 differences. **Are the differences close?** If students say yes, tell them their answer is reasonable.
- Have partners take turns solving several more problems.

13•13 ADD AND SUBTRACT MONEY AMOUNTS

Materials: envelopes, play dollars and coins
- Give each student an envelope with an amount of money between $2.50 and $4.99 and a sheet of paper.
- Have students work in pairs. Tell partners to count the money in their envelopes and write the amount at the top of their paper. (Write $3.98 on the chalkboard as a model for writing a money amount.) Have each partner tell the other how much money he or she has. Have each partner write this amount under their original amount. Have partners add the two amounts. Ask if their sums are the same. *yes*
- Have partners use the same 2 original amounts and subtract the lesser amount from the greater amount.

Name _____ Date _____

Using a Bar Graph to Solve a Problem

Cut out the parts of the bar graph.

Paste each part where it belongs.

Use the graph to solve a problem.

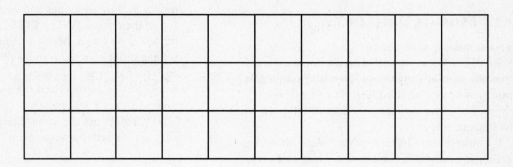

| 0 | 5 | 10 | 15 | 20 | 25 | 30 | 35 | 40 | 45 | 50 |

Number of stamps

New Stamps

| Kinds of stamps | flowers | people | birds |

CHAPTER 14 Multiplication and Division

Objectives

- skip count to find how many in all
- use repeated addition or multiplication
- use arrays to write multiplication sentences
- multiply across and down
- multiply factors in any order
- make predictions to solve a problem

Cluster A Materials

- connecting cubes, counters, or dried beans
- index cards cut in half
- small paper cups
- Activity Page 14-A

Math Words

Words	Examples
array	Show a sample **array** of 4 rows of circles with 2 circles in each row.
factors	4 x 2 = 8
multiply	4 groups x 2 in each group = 8 in all
multiplication sentence	4 x 2 = 8
product	4 x 2 = 8

Teaching Strategies See pp. v–vi for teaching tips on working with ELL students.

14•1 SKIP COUNTING

Materials: for each student: 10 small paper cups, 30 connecting cubes, counters, or dried beans

- Have students arrange 6 cups in a row and put 2 cubes in each cup. **How many cubes did you use in all?** *12* Invite a volunteer to demonstrate how he or she counted the cubes.
- Tell students that they can skip count to find how many. Ask students to skip count aloud by 2s to 12. You may wish to display a number line and point to each number as students skip count.

- Next, have students arrange 5 cups in a row and put 5 cubes in each cup. Have them skip count aloud by 5s to find how many cubes in all. *25*
- Repeat with 3 cups and 10 cubes in each cup, 10 cups and 2 cubes in each cup, and so on.

14•2 REPEATED ADDITION AND MULTIPLICATION

Materials: index cards cut in half, 6 small paper cups, 12 connecting cubes, counters, or dried beans

- Distribute materials to pairs of students. Have partners arrange 3 cups in a row and put 4 cubes in each cup. Have partners then skip count to find how many in all.
- Explain that because each cup has the same number of cubes, students can use repeated addition to find how many in all. Have one partner write 4, +, 4, +, 4, =, and 12 on index cards and arrange them to make an addition sentence to tell about the cups of cubes. Have partners read aloud the number sentence.
- Explain that they can also use multiplication. **How many groups of cubes do you have?** *3* **How many cubes in each group?** *4* Have the other partner write 3, ×, 4, =, and 12 on index cards. Help partners to arrange the cards to make a multiplication sentence and to read it aloud.
- Have partners repeat the activity with 6 cups of 2 beans, 4 cups of 3 beans, and 2 cups of 6 beans.

14•3 USE ARRAYS

Materials: index cards cut in half

- Distribute 12 cards to each student. Write 4 × 3 = 12 on the chalkboard and ask what it is. *a multiplication sentence* Have students say the sentence with you.
- Invite students to use the cards to show the multiplication sentence by making 4 rows of 3 cards. As students complete the task, check their work by having them count the rows and cards in each row.
- Tell students they have just made an array. Write *array* on the chalkboard and have students say the word. Focus attention on students' arrays and number sentence. **What does the 4 tell you?** *number of rows* **What does the 3 tell you?** *how many per row* **What does the 12 tell you?** *how many in all*
- Have students make other arrays to show these sentences: 2 × 6 = 12, 6 × 2 = 12, 1 × 12 = 12, and 3 × 4 = 12.

14•4 MULTIPLICATION

Materials: index cards cut in half
- Distribute 15–20 cards to pairs of students. Have partners make an array of 3 rows of 4 cards each. **What multiplication sentence tells what you did?** *3 × 4 = 12* Write the sentence on the chalkboard. **What does the sentence mean?** *3 groups of 4 equal 12* Write *factor × factor = product* under the sentence. As you point to each number, have students read the word.
- Write *3 × 4 = 12* in vertical form, as you explain to students that they can also multiply down. Ask students to name the factors and product as you point to each number. **How are the two ways alike and different?** *They have the same factors and multiplication symbol; the products are the same; one has an equal symbol, the other has a line.*
- Have partners take turns making different arrays. When one partner makes an array, have the other partner write and solve the fact two ways.

14•5 MORE MULTIPLICATION

Materials: index cards cut in half, Activity Page 14-A
- Distribute an activity page and 20 cards to each student. Have students form pairs. Ask one partner to show an array of 4 groups of 5 and the other to show an array of 5 groups of 4. **What multiplication sentences tell what you did?** *4 × 5 = 20, 5 × 4 = 20* Write the sentences on the chalkboard. **How are the 2 alike and different?** *The factors and products are the same; the order of the factors is different.*
- Continue by having partners make the following arrays: 2 groups of 10; 10 groups of 2; 3 groups of 6; 6 groups of 3; 3 groups of 5; 5 groups of 3. For each set, have partners draw the 2 arrays on their activity pages and the multiplication sentence to tell about each one.

14•6 READING FOR MATH: MAKE A PREDICTION

Materials: connecting cubes
- Write the following problem on the chalkboard: **Miss Lee asks 5 students to help carry books to the library. Jana has 6 books. Sam, Ed, Tina, and Luis each carry the same number of books. Predict how many books the students carry altogether.**
- **What do you want to find out?** *how many books in all the students take to the library* **What do you know?** *the number of students; how many books each one carries* **How many students help?** *5* **How many books does each student carry?** *6 books* Call on volunteers to underline the sentences with these facts. Then, have students predict the number of books the students carry in all. Record their predictions on the chalkboard.
- Have students show how they would go about verifying their predictions using multiplication and modeling with connecting cubes or by acting it out.

Activity Page 14-A

Name _____   Date _____

Exploring Multiplication with Arrays

Draw each array you make. Draw each array your
partner makes.

Write a multiplication sentence to tell about each one.

_____

What do the arrays and multiplication sentences show?

_____

```
┌─────────────────────┐   ┌─────────────────────┐
│                     │   │                     │
│                     │   │                     │
│                     │   │                     │
│                     │   │                     │
│                     │   │                     │
└─────────────────────┘   └─────────────────────┘
```

_____ × _____ = _____   _____ × _____ = _____

```
┌─────────────────────┐   ┌─────────────────────┐
│                     │   │                     │
│                     │   │                     │
│                     │   │                     │
│                     │   │                     │
│                     │   │                     │
└─────────────────────┘   └─────────────────────┘
```

_____ × _____ = _____   _____ × _____ = _____

```
┌─────────────────────┐   ┌─────────────────────┐
│                     │   │                     │
│                     │   │                     │
│                     │   │                     │
│                     │   │                     │
│                     │   │                     │
└─────────────────────┘   └─────────────────────┘
```

_____ × _____ = _____   _____ × _____ = _____

Cluster B, pages 529-538

Objectives

- draw a picture to solve problems
- use repeated subtraction to divide into equal groups
- relate division and repeated subtraction
- make equal groups
- divide with remainders

Cluster B Materials

- connecting cubes
- dried beans
- paper plates (white and a contrasting color)
- small paper cups
- Activity Page 14-B

Math Words

Words	Examples
divide	Demonstrate how to divide a group of 6 items into 2 groups of 3 items.
division sentence	$6 \div 2 = 3$
quotient	$6 \div 2 = 3$
remainder	Show a group of 9 items divided into 2 groups of 4 with 1 item left over

Teaching Strategies See pp. v–vi for teaching tips on working with ELL students.

14•7 Problem Solving Strategy: Draw a Picture

- Write this problem on the chalkboard: **A group of children fill 5 boxes. Each box holds 9 cans. How many cans do they pack in all?** Have students read the problem. **What do you know?** *how many boxes; how many cans fit in each box* **What do you want to find out?** *how many cans the children pack in all*
- Tell students they can draw a picture to help solve the problem. **What will you draw?** *5 boxes, 9 cans in each box* **What will you do next?** *multiply* After drawing a picture, have students write a multiplication sentence to solve the problem. **How did drawing a picture help you?**

14•8 Repeated Subtraction

Materials: for each pair of students: 6 small paper cups, 20 dried beans

- Distribute materials to partners. Ask one partner to count out 12 beans, subtract 3, and put them in a cup. Ask the other partner to write a subtraction sentence to show what his or her partner did. *12 – 3 = 9* As the one partner continues subtracting 3 beans at a time, putting each set in a new cup, have the other partner write a subtraction sentence for each action. *9 – 3 = 6, 6 – 3 = 3, 3 – 3 = 0* **How many equal groups do you have?** *4 equal groups of 3*
- Have partners switch roles to show and write repeated subtraction sentences as follows: starting with 20 counters and subtracting 5 at a time, 18 counters and subtracting 3 at a time, 16 counters and subtracting 4 at a time, and so on.

14•9 Subtraction and Division

Materials: small paper cups, dried beans, Activity Page 14-B

- Distribute materials to partners. Have one partner count out 12 beans, subtract groups of 2, putting each group in a different cup, as the other partner records each subtraction. **How many equal groups of 2 do you have?** *6* **How many times did you subtract?** *6* Write on the chalkboard 12 – 2 = 10, 10 – 2 = 8, 8 – 2 = 6, and so on.
- Tell students they can also write a division sentence to show what they did. Write 12 ÷ 2 = 6 **How many beans did you start with?** *12* **How many beans did you put in each group?** *2* **How many equal groups of 2 did you make?** *6* **How many times did you subtract?** *6 times* Point to the 6 subtraction sentences. Then, point to the quotient. **What do you notice about the quotient in the division sentence and the number of times you subtracted?** *They are the same.*
- Have partners continue exploring subtraction and division on the activity page. Have them make equal groups of 3 and 4, writing subtraction sentences and a division sentence for each, and drawing a picture.

14•10 Division

Materials: white paper plates, paper plates of a contrasting color cut into 12 equal "pizza slices"

- Distribute 6 paper plates and 12 "pizza slices" to each student. **If you and a friend are sharing the pizza equally, how many slices do you each get?** *6* Have students divide the slices into 2 equal groups on 2 paper plates. Tell students that if they put 6 slices on each of the 2 plates, then they and their friend each have a fair share.
- Have students show how they would divide the pizza slices with 2 friends, 3 friends, and 5 friends. Remind

students not to forget themselves when dividing. As you check students' work, ask questions such as **How many plates do you need for you and 2 friends (3 friends, 5 friends)? How do you know if each person has a fair share?**

14•11 MORE DIVISION

Materials: connecting cubes

- Give each student 20 connecting cubes. Have them connect 6 cubes and then make as many more equal groups of 6 as they can. **How many equal groups of 6** did you make? *3* **Do you have any cubes left over?** *yes* **How many?** *2* Write *remainder* on the chalkboard, explaining that 2 is the remainder when they divided 20 into 3 equal groups of 6.

- Have students divide 20 cubes into as many equal groups of 4 as they can. Repeat the questions. **How many equal groups of 4 did you make?** *5* **Do you have any cubes left over?** *no*

- Continue by having students divide 20 cubes in as many equal groups of 3, 4, 7, 8, 9, and 10 as they can, each time telling how many equal groups they made and any remainder they have.

Activity Page 14-B

Name _____ Date _____

Exploring the Subtraction and Division Connection

Draw the number of beans you start with each time.

Circle the beans to show each equal group you make.

Write the subtraction sentences.

Write a division sentence.

1. Equal groups of 3

_____ - _____ = _____

_____ - _____ = _____

_____ - _____ = _____   or   _____ ÷ _____ = _____

_____ - _____ = _____

2. Equal groups of 4

_____ - _____ = _____

_____ - _____ = _____   or   _____ ÷ _____ = _____

_____ - _____ = _____

Activity Page 1-A
1. $4 + 3 = 7$; $3 + 4 = 7$
2. $2 + 6 = 8$; $6 + 2 = 8$
3. $5 + 4 = 9$; $4 + 5 = 9$
4. $8 + 2 = 10$; $2 + 8 = 10$
5. $9 + 3 = 12$; $3 + 9 = 12$

Activity Page 1-B
Students' drawings should show 9 ladybugs.
$5 + 4 = 9$

Activity Page 2-A
Check students' drawings.

5 books and 7 more books $5 + 7 = 12$

Activity Page 2-B
Answers will vary.

Activity Page 3-A
Answers will vary.

Activity Page 3-B
For Activity 3•10: Check students' work. The colored number squares should show the pattern for counting by 2s, 3s, 4s, or 5s.

For Activity 3•11: Check students' placement of cubes or counters.

Activity Page 4-A
46¢: 1 quarter, 2 dimes, 1 penny; 4 coins

58¢: 1 half dollar, 1 nickel, 3 pennies; 5 coins

63¢: 1 half dollar, 1 dime, 3 pennies; 5 coins

78¢: 1 half dollar, 1 quarter, 3 pennies; 5 coins

82¢: 1 half dollar, 1 quarter, 1 nickel, 2 pennies; 5 coins

99¢: 1 half dollar, 1 quarter, 2 dimes, 4 pennies; 8 coins

Activity Page 4-B
3 dimes; 2 dimes and 2 nickels; 1 dime, 4 nickels; 6 nickels

Activity Page 5-A
Answers will vary.

Activity Page 5-B
1. 16 yellow flowers;
   18 red flowers
2. how many flowers in all
3. Check students' drawings.
4. The children picked 34 flowers in all.

Activity Page 6-A
Answers will vary.

Activity Page 6-B
1. 22¢
2. 16¢
3. 7¢
4. 9¢

Activity Page 7-A
1. 5:40
   40 minutes after 5
   20 minutes before 6
2. 11:15
   quarter after 11
   45 minutes before 12
   15 minutes after 11

Activity Page 7-B
Answers will vary.

Activity Page 8-A
Bar graph title: Favorite Seasons (or similar)

Summer: 9 squares should be filled in

Fall: 4 squares should be filled in

Winter: 7 squares should be filled in

Spring: 6 squares should be filled in

Activity Page 8-B
Check that each bar graph correctly reflects the data on the "Our Favorite Subjects" tally table completed for Activity 8•2.

Activity Page 9-A
Answers will vary.

Activity Page 9-B
Answers will vary. Check students' temperature readings and drawings.

Activity Page 10-A
Check that students match each shape with the correct label.

Activity Page 10-B
Figures will vary. Check that both parts match.

Activity Page 11-A
Check that students color in 1 part of each rectangle and correctly write the fraction for each part: $\frac{1}{2}$; $\frac{1}{4}$, $\frac{1}{8}$, $\frac{1}{3}$, $\frac{1}{6}$, $\frac{1}{12}$.

Activity Page 11-B
Answers will vary.

Activity Page 12-A
Answers will vary.

Activity Page 12-B
Answers will vary.

Activity Page 13-A
Answers will vary.

Activity Page 13-B

Check that students have filled in the correct number of squares to show 38 flower stamps, 21 bird stamps, and 29 famous people stamps.

Activity Page 14-A

Check students' arrays and sentences.

1. $2 \times 10 = 20; 10 \times 2 = 20$ 3. $3 \times 5 = 15; 5 \times 3 = 15$
2. $3 \times 6 = 18; 6 \times 3 = 18$

You can multiply the same factors in any order.

Activity Page 14-B

1. $12 - 3 = 9$
   $9 - 3 = 6$
   $6 - 3 = 3$
   $3 - 3 = 0$
   $12 \div = 4$

2. $12 - 4 = 8$
   $8 - 4 = 4$
   $4 - 4 = 0$
   $12 \div 4 = 3$

Teacher Notes

Teacher Notes